A NEW WIFE IN THE SUN

One Foot in the Brave

Paula Leskovitz

Wandering Woman

From a very young age you used to tell me stories before bedtime. Not ones pulled off a bookshelf, but original tales created by your own vivid imagination. One story I remember more than any other was called 'The Magic Stick'.

This useless piece of driftwood used to chase robbers down the road and reprimand bullies, but this stick when asked to perform on demand would never adhere; it would remain immobile and inert.

I'm a little like that stick, I refuse to conform and I have you to thank for that.

This book is dedicated to you mum, you are my favourite story teller of all time.

CONTENTS

A NEW WIFE IN THE SUN

By Paula Leskovitz

PROLOGUE

April 2018

My husband finally admitted defeat after being force fed 'A Place in the Sun' throughout several rain swept British months.

In the revelationary episode, Aunt Maude had left a substantial inheritance to a lacklustre middle aged couple who, after being shown several stunning Spanish properties on the Andalucían coast, suddenly decided they wanted to stay in their two up two down in damp and dreary Oswaldtwistle as opposed to a beachside penthouse. Shaking my head in disgust I pointed my rapidly disintegrating nobbly bobbly towards my ever weary spouse who appeared to be feigning sleep to avoid my daily ramblings about factor 50.

"I'm telling you, come 2019 we won't even be able to move to Europe! All our freedom will be ripped away from us and we're going have to stay in this bloody godforsaken town with its crappy weather forever!"

Brushing a wayward vanilla dribble off my increasingly expanding belly I sighed dramatically and haul myself off the sofa and sulkily stared out of the kitchen window at the grey clouds rolling heavily across the November sky.

Opening one wary eye whilst simultaneously rubbing away the deeply ingrained London smog from his daily commute, the man I married only 7 years earlier raised his hands in a 'you win' gesture and uttered the words I'd been longing to hear since we tied the knot in Vegas aided by a man in bell bottoms and raven black hair.

"For god's sake, if you stop bleating on about it we'll sell up and move, but you have the honor of informing everyone of our plans, and that includes my mum!"

Removing my disbelieving jaw from the fading Axmister I screamed in excitement and scrambled over to the ancient laptop to compare the price of international schools and what paperwork is legally required for back-packing hounds. Behind me I can hear my husband mumbling under his breath about Rabies jabs and how they are missing a trick by not administering them to menopausal housewives with ADHD.

Looking down at the family dog I make a mental note to contact the vets to get his miniature maracas removed before heading off on our midlife adventure. The last thing I needed on my sun drenched balcony was the pitter patter of several tiny hairy feet after a canine night out on the tiles. (I did actually enquire with the family GP if the same procedure could be done with my slightly younger husband but amazingly, I have to have his consent first).

So here I find myself, exactly 5 months down the line and one week shy of my 51st birthday, staring excitedly out of the giant airport windows and into the unknown. Beside me my twelve year old son mumbles something incoherent about Mozzarella and donuts then ambles off to purchase a baguette which costs roughly the same price as my first car. The boy child is more than happy to relocate abroad. He's watched reruns of Bay Watch. He's acutely aware that everyone on a sandy beach runs in slow motion and looks like Pamela Anderson. Also to soften the blow I've bribed him with the promise of several new Xbox games (yes I am a bad parent, but at least I'll be a bad parent in a vest as opposed to a cardi).

The house is under offer, the farewell tears have been shed. Man and mutt are loaded up in the newly purchased Jeep, our worldly possessions crammed into every available crevice. No doubt by now both of them will be cascading over the French border, happily singing Charles Aznavour tunes en route to Paris. The ties with normality have been cut, my televised dream is about to become a reality.

I glance down at the battered suitcase in my hand and grip the one way ticket to Malaga tightly in my pale fist. We have no home, we have no jobs, and we don't speak Spanish. We are either very brave or very stupid or just very naive.

Taking a deep breath I drag my belongings and my monosyllabic child towards the open gate which is now apparently boarding. This is the moment our lives will change forever. I smile inwardly and pull my big girl pants up a little higher. Waving goodbye to normality I put my best foot forward and take the first intrepid step towards our new life in the sun.

ONE FOOT IN
THE BRAVE

"**M**um, would you rather die by being sucked down the toilet, rammed by the drinks trolley or catapulted out the window?"

Ignoring the boy child's Haribo infused fascination with morbid in-flight endings; I fasten my seatbelt and look out the window at the country I still call home. Catching my own reflexion in the glass I see my mother's eyes looking back at me and I wonder if I've made the right decision by letting my husband drive all the way to Spain. Tears prickle behind my eyes and I rapidly blink them back. I really hope he hasn't crashed travelling through France as I've grown quite fond of that glass coffee table he's got bubble wrapped in the boot.

Anyone thinking about relocating to Spain will find long term accommodation hard to come by, especially in the tourist resorts as the summer season approaches but I have been fortunate enough to be put in touch with a friend of a friend's auntie's brother's great niece who has inherited a family house in the Campo which we can stay in rent free as long as my husband promises to repair a few electrical bits and tidies the garden occasionally. I don't quite know what a Campo is but it all sounds very glam and Poldark esque. I'm consumed by visions of myself riding bareback to the local fruit and veg market on an untamed Palomino stallion. Hundreds of Looky-Looky men follow my progression through the various stalls as I scoop up several kilos of sundried tomatoes and casually drop them onto my rotating umbrella hat. In reality, I'd probably have to tuck my breasts into my knickers if I rode anything that went any faster than a slow amble in fear of giving myself a black eye.

Time flies like my transient youth and before I have time to order another vodka chaser we have crossed countries, breezed through customs and are tucked safely on board the fast train to Fuengirola. Unfortunately most of the 35 minute journey is spent apologizing to the local residents as our errant Suitcases decide to take on a Torvil & Dean style skate off down the centre aisle every time the train departs a station. Straddling both bags with my fluorescent thighs I smile apologetically at our captive olive skinned audience and they shake their heads in weary acceptance at the anemic interlopers currently invading not only their network system but their country too.

On exiting the train station we rapidly locate the taxi rank and I bang on the window of several sleepy drivers who take one look at the hastily scribbled accommodation address and shake their heads in a no nonsense manner. Finally one elderly chap nods in agreement and looks dramatically up towards the hills. Without further adieu our bags are hurled into his boot and with his foot on the gas he indicates Left, promptly turns right and without even a nod to the wing mirror, takes an unscheduled u-turn in the road.

Within minutes we are gliding up the A7 motorway through the

Costa del Sol. Bleached villas envelop the landscape either side of the road and Indigo Pools twinkle in the afternoon sunlight. Heading towards a sign that reads 'La Cala de Mijas' we leave the familiarity of the road and head North onto a dirt track which appears to lead upwards into oblivion. My adventurer's spirit rapidly starts to fade as we climb higher and higher into the mountains until the only thing left to view is the horizon. Thunder rolls overhead and the Sun is eclipsed by a cloud the colour of granite. We turn one final corner and come to an abrupt stop in front of a fenced off compound surrounding a rather ramshackle wooden house that wouldn't look out of place in a Freddy Krueger sequel.

The driver drops our luggage by the fence and disappears in a cloud of dust. My son shields his eyes and squints towards our new abode and then enquiringly back at me. I smile encouragingly and head towards the padlocked gate but his voice stops me instantly in my tracks.

"I really don't want to worry you mother but there's a very large goat about to eat my suitcase"

ONLY GOATS
AND HORSES

O blivious to the correct protocol when one is faced with a suitcase eating goat, I did what I thought Bear Grylls would do in this situation; I wrestled it to the ground, chopped it up into bite size pieces and turned it into a nice curry.

Obviously that's a lie; I'm not actually that keen on curry, so I yelled and shook my hand luggage at the uninvited guest while my son hid behind the nearest bush. Both kids stared at me for a moment, and then the hairier of the two grew bored and decided to relocate to the field opposite, gripping the severed handle of the aforementioned case like a well deserved trophy and promptly disappeared into the brush.

Without further ado, I unlocked the gate, ran through, slammed it shut, heard more yelling, remembered I had a son, let him in, slammed it shut for a second time and made a bid for the safe confines of the house. After a brief knee shuffle we located the keys which were hidden under the BBQ and without further interruption we entered our new temporary home.

Leaning with my back against the closed door I searched for the light and flicked the switch. Several lamps erupted into life, illuminating a warm and welcoming lounge and kitchen area. My son, all thoughts of our wildlife interlude forgotten, ran upstairs to the largest of the four double bedrooms and threw his bag onto the floor and promptly set about finding out where the WIFI code was located. I on the other hand looked for the most important item in the house, the kettle.

After a brief sanity respite containing three sugars and an out of date chocolate bourbon, I finally took stock of our surroundings. The house was completely made of wood, not a brick in sight. An arsonists dream. I trailed my hand against the warm grain and dragged my weary legs upstairs in search of the bathroom. Post wee and wash I wandered down the hall and flopped down onto the first available bed I came to. Without invitation oblivion engulfed me and drifted off into a much welcomed late afternoon siesta.

Just as I was happily chatting away to the tin man about the liberal use of WD40, Dorothy rudely interrupted our conversation by yelling something about not being in Kansas anymore. It was at that point the bed beneath me decided to vibrate, and may I add, not in an entirely pleasant way.

I opened one eye to make sure the ruby slippers were still adorning my trotters when the house was suddenly engulfed in a bright light. Boy child, headphones surgically attached to his head launched himself into my room, almost taking the door off its hinges in the process yelling 'This is your fault, I knew we should have stayed at the premier inn, this place is haunted!' and then jumped onto the bed beside me and dived under the covers all the while mumbling about crucifixes and rotating heads. Rubbing the sleep from my eyes I looked around the room and at that point another flash of light erupted from behind the curtain followed by an enormous thunder clap. An involuntary yelp seeped out from under the covers followed by a faint whisper

"Take her, she's older and an atheist".

Staggering from the bed I headed over towards the window and pulled back the blinds. A massive electrical storm was cascading down around us with forked lightning dancing over the sea, causing the house to shake like a 6th grader at his first prom. Opening the balcony door I walked out onto the decking and stood in awe watching Mother Nature conduct her own impromptu light show.

A series of knocks on the front door dragged me back into reality and I stumbled onto the landing and peered around the banister. A tall silhouette stood outside in the dark, hunched against the door frame with his back to the glass, a sack slung over his shoulder. Holding a finger to my lips I motioned to my son to be quiet. The stranger banged on the door again, this time more forceful and I stood still, rooted to the spot with fear, all thoughts of lazy days in the sun fading like a distant memory. Taking a deep breath I steeled another look around the corner, heart in mouth to see the intruder looking directly at me, hair plastered to his head but with strangely familiar eyes.

'Are you going to bloody let me in or not? I've not had a decent cuppa in over a 1000 miles?'

DARLING BUDS
OF PREY

My husband, coated in mud, is standing on my doorstep which is actually physically impossible unless he is the latest companion of Tom Baker. Pressing my face up against the window I look for a Blue Police Box but all I can see is the velvet sky. The man I'm married only left the UK with our ancient Jeep this morning and as far as I am aware, time travel was not mentioned once in our courtship. I take a step back and rub my eyes. This dream is extremely realistic; I can even feel the wooden floor creaking beneath my toes as I head back up the stairs to bed.

"Mum, stop being a div, let dad in! He text me and asked me to keep it a secret. He didn't leave Hastings this morning; he left yesterday afternoon after dropping us off at that crappy Gatwick hotel. While we were sleeping he was driving across France!"

I stop dead in my tracks and turn around. Brian, the dog is standing outside next to his jaded master, wagging his tail and looking wistfully up at the door handle. I decide to throw caution to the wind and let both apparitions in. The hairy one greets me with his usual kisses and slobbers gratefully over my outstretched hand but I hastily avoid the lips of my spouse as he smells distinctly of stale coffee and animal poo. It transpires that on entering the drive, my other half tripped over several dozing goats and went face first into their ablutions. I try not to laugh and fail dismally.

Placating the man child with a mug of something hot and sweet I spend the following 30 minutes running around after our dog that appears intent on weeing on every piece of wood in the house.

After the men folk are showered I manage to find some pasta and a red sauce in the cupboard and throw together a meat free Bolognese that for once, no-one complains about. Bleary eyed and slightly delirious we all head upstairs to bed, exhilarated and exhausted in equal measures.

I am awoken just before the sun has chance to rise by the sound of several dogs barking, 403 birds singing, a Rooster yelling and a husband snoring. Turning to look at my watch I see it's almost 6am. Lying in bed looking at the ceiling I decide it's no use even attempting to go back to sleep so I head downstairs to put the kettle on.

The sun is streaming through the windows and I open the patio doors to let the dog out and the warm breeze in. Stretching, Brian heads outside and sniffs the air and ambles off into the brush. Seconds later he is back indoors and hiding under the table. I cajole him out with a biscuit and he stands shivering, staring at the brush and wining, Hobnob untouched. I drag my flip flops on and go out to investigate as to why a hound that should be programmed to round up sheep is currently trying to crawl under the fridge.

I wander the perimeter, gently humming to myself. I shake my head and smile, there's absolutely nothing here to be afraid of, that dog is as yellow as.... oh!

Mingled in amongst the weeds is a tiny tortoiseshell kitten. Only something isn't quite right. I take a step back and tilt my chin. It takes a few seconds to realise what's wrong with the tiny corpse. It has no head, just a little furry body of about 8 weeks old. It's 6am, I've not even had anything with caffeine in and already I'm staring at a decapitated pussy. I look around and instantly I see another striped body further down the embankment. This one has its head intact but is also motionless. Within seconds I spot another sibling, also dead with puncture marks to its chest. Three dead cats. It's like a sadistic nursery rhyme penned by a juvenile Steven King. I stagger back into the house and pelt up the stairs to awake my sleeping partner.

"Marcus... MARCUS!! There are three dead cats in the garden and one has no head!!!'

My husband, never the earliest of risers mumbles something about Winona Ryder, laughs, farts and promptly starts snoring again. I sigh; shake my head and return downstairs in search of some gardening gloves, resigned to my task ahead.

And so, this is how you will find me at 6.13am on a sunny Saturday morning. I'm the slightly overweight middle aged woman staggering about on the gravel drive clad in an 'I love Disco' Onesie, clutching a bin bag in one hand and a trowel in the other. It wasn't the welcome I expected on my first morning in Spain but it's one I certainly won't forget. Now if you will excuse me, I have three small bodies to bury.

TO BE OR NOT TO BE, THAT IS THE GREEN ROOM

So here we are, our family of four, finally living in Spain. I actually can't quite believe it. The dream we never thought would happen is now our reality. And unfortunately, reality involves getting a job.

Having met my husband at the local Am Dram society in Hastings several years (and dress sizes) earlier, I decided to make contact before leaving the UK with the Fuengirola equivalent known as the 'Salon Varieties Theatre'. After peddling my wares on Face Book messenger, I happened to mention that my husband is an electrician and they replied forthwith explaining that their lighting technician was about to retire in April and would my husband be interested in applying for the position? Bears and woods instantly spring to mind.

Now, before I go any further, can we briefly talk about 'Dream Jobs'? We all have that one thing we would love to do for a living. I'd love to write a book. A book that you can hold in your hand, to sniff the ageing paper, to turn over the corner of the page when your eyes grow weary and laugh out loud in a room full of people and not care because for that brief moment in time, you are that heroine in chapter 12.

To see my name on a dust cover would be better than waking up without pillow marks embedded onto my crepe face.

My husband's school leaving wish was to work in the West End, to bring the performers to life in front of a live audience. With his dream still intact he escaped the clutches of the local secondary modern age 16, gangly and unprepared, suited and booted, innocent and eager in front of the careers advisor who instantly poured water on his ambitions by replying "No son, that's a career for fantasists and rich people from London. Get yourself a proper job. People will always need plugs and sockets and wires changing. Become an electrician, you'll always be able to put food on the table then".

So that's what he did 30 years ago, he became an electrician. A job he enjoyed but never loved. And now, on offer, in a resort 1300 miles away is a chance to turn back the clock. So, after a brief 'we're here!' call, off we trot, showered and shaved (and that's just me) to meet the people that have the potential to re-instate a young man's dreams on an a slightly jaded body.

An hour later we are sat outside the Theatre bar, drinking fresh orange juice and waiting with sweaty palms to meet 'the board members'. The tables surrounding the thespian haven are adorned with middle-aged laughing people. Men with perma-tans, women with white teeth, everyone appears happy in their skin and at ease with their choice. A mixture of Spanglish echoes around us and I whisper to my husband to stop jigging his legs up and down, this was a job he had done voluntarily on his own time for the past three decades; the only difference now is that he would be paid to do it this time round.

A firm hand is placed on my shoulder and I look up into welcoming brown eyes.

'So, you must be the power behind the throne!' laughs the stranger in my direction and introduces himself and also what his role is on the board and finally, what would be expected if Marcus was given the job. An older lady joins him and warmly kisses me on each cheek. Both members talk passionately about their time in the British speaking Theatre then lead us through velvet clad stage doors into a hub of adrenalin filled activity.

On stage a rehearsal is taking place. Young and old high kick their way into the wings while a director booms instructions from the front row of the auditorium. I look up at the lights and breathe in the smell of the greasepaint. Teenagers with languid expressions awaiting their time in the spotlight come to life as they are released from the confines of backstage and leap like adrenalin fuelled antelopes onto the well trodden boards.

Turning to my husband I smile but he is lost within the lighting control desk, eyes alight with all the possibilities ahead akin to Mr. Spock faced with the new and updated Starship Enterprise. I look towards the man and the woman who greeted us on arrival; both look at ease with the roles they have been given in order to keep this well preserved British Galleon afloat in a Spanish ocean.

The man senses my gaze and leans against the door. 'So what are you going to do for work here?' He asks enquiringly? Before my brain has time to engage with my mouth my truth tourettes steps in to reply on my behalf

"In all honesty... I have absolutely no bloody idea"

He laughs and nods his heads towards my husband

"Well, the job's his if he wants it, his references are excellent, and I think you'll both fit in well here, what you think?"

I look him in the eye and smile and reply on behalf of my whole theatrical family

"Sir, I think we'd both like that very much"

FROM HAIR TO ETERNITY

So within the first 72 hours of being in the Costa del Sol, my husband has bagged a sought after contracted job and is up bright and early the following morning to begin his first day at the Theatre. I drop him off in the town centre and he cheerily waves goodbye whilst clutching his Minions Lunch box and a bag of Spanners.

I turn and look at my son, paint on an enthusiastic smile and take a deep breath.

"Soooo, are you ready to go look at some schools???" I say in an overconfident voice. He looks at me out of the corner of his eye and mumbles "yeah... but only if we get that Xbox game you promised me"

So on this sunny day, less than a week into our adventure, mother and son spend a warm afternoon visiting several international schools up and down the Mijas coast and by 5pm we have agreed on a small college situated in the centre of Fuengirola. The deciding factor for the boy child is that it is based underneath a water park but for me, it's the fact that there are only 14 children in the class. The lady at reception smiles and swipes my credit card as I wince at the amount leaving our account. I console myself with the fact that Private education costs more than double this back in the UK then hastily head outside into the street to hyperventilate into a McDonalds take away bag.

With reality sitting firmly on my shoulders, I plonk my ample buttocks on a nearby bench and look up at the orange blossom casting shadows across the pavement. Husband and son have a clear path towards their future in this foreign land and suddenly, for the first time on this journey into the unknown, I begin to think about me. What am I going to do work wise here to enable us to fund our new life in the sun? I'm 51, hardly the age to re-train as a stripper in 24 hour square. I glance across to adjacent shop window selling opaque mirrors and reflect on the choices I have made in my life. I close my eyes and see my younger self with these new opportunities, what would she have done with them? My eyelids grow heavy with the weight of responsibility and...

...its 1983, I'm 16 years of age, my breasts are unfeasibly pert and the biggest decision I have to make in life is what flavour lip gloss to wear. Exactly one month after leaving school with only two 'O' levels to my name, my mother threatens to throw all my Heaven 17 albums away unless I tidy up my bedroom and more importantly, for her

middle aged sanity, find myself a job. Begrudgingly I browse through the local newspaper and spot an advert for an apprentice hairdresser. The wage is £29 a week and all the hair lacquer I can hide down my trouser leg. After a brief interview with the weary weight watching female owner of the salon I am offered the post of chief tea maker and sweeper upper. A jubilant mother cooks me Faggots and Peas to celebrate my impending foray into adulthood.

The enforced career choice isn't exactly the most demanding job in the world. My best creative work at the salon is invariably performed the morning after the night before. On one occasion, an elderly clients hair is removed unceremoniously from her scalp alongside the rubber streaking cap after applying the wrong volume peroxide onto an already over processed head. Needless to say my wages for that week are consumed on a selection of head scarves for the irate customer in question. Undeterred and unrepentant I promise my jaded employer I will take the position more seriously from this day forth but come 6pm I'm sprinting home to change into my tucker books and Lady Di blouse, all promises forgotten, the disco beckons.

With Spam sandwich firmly in hand, my girlfriends and I jump on the bus and spend the one hour journey in silence, looking through the dirty windows, our New Romantic souls tortured with yearning over which Duranie is the most delectable. After reaching our destination we smile coyly at the doormen and are granted permission to enter, our blossoming bodies the only entrance fee we have to pay. Youth is a commodity and we barter well. The hours pass by, fuelled by Malibu and Coke and Marlboro lights. Smiling and flirting, we sway in time to the music, taking it in turns to work the dance floor knowing that eventually we will locate a proud male owner of a coveted Ford Capri who will happily chauffeur us all back to our beds at 2am and all we have to do in exchange for this free transportation is provide flattery and broken promises. We are young, we are beautiful, we are...

..."Mum, have you nodded off??" yells a familiar voice in my ear.

I bolt upright, wiping a dab of dribble off my chin, my nubile younger self is nothing but a distant memory and the reality of the present is facing me with hands on hips.

"Of course not" I blurt out, whilst trying to stand up on my recently awakened legs.

"Well that's good because while you were having your lady nap I've been looking on Google and there's a Game shop just down the road. And I'm really hungry, can we have some KFC?"

Just then the phone rings. Husband is ready to be picked up from work. He's hungry too.

I sigh and nod my head and make my way towards the car. Tomorrow I will start to think about what I want out of our impending adventure but right now, the only thing I really desire is the Colonels secret recipe along with a side order of bravery and the courage of my younger self.

ANOTHER BRIT
IN THE WALL

B efore we left the UK to reside in Spain I enjoyed nothing more than a good old moan about the country I was born in.

I knotted my eyebrows and ranted to my ageing neighbours, bemoaning how all the decent high street shops were now empty and abandoned but then on returning indoors to the sanctity of my home I suddenly realized that everything I'd ordered this Christmas was from Amazon online, I'd bought nothing locally.

I regaled anyone that cared enough to listen upon the decline of decent job opportunities for the over forties but then conveniently failed to mention that I'd quit my previous employment because the obligatory nylon uniform was itchy and unflattering and the hours unsociable.

I bemoaned the fact that not one of my Carol Vorderman inspired dresses fitted around my middle aged torso anymore but then consoled my aching heart with a Grints Sausage roll and a can of Cream Soda.

But the topic I loved moaning about most, my favourite subject of all time, was of course the British weather.

I genuinely think the Government should declare the 15th of August a National public holiday in the UK. We could name it 'I've moaned all winter that I'm frozen but now I'm too hot and can't fit in my shorts or use a hosepipe' day.

But NONE of the above things can even walk in the shadow of the biggest Spanish contender, the Muhammad Ali of anguish and stress in your local region of choice; ladies and gentlemen I give you the Numero uno subject of strife here amidst the expats … local bureaucracy!

Let me elaborate. As an employed person with a contract, my husband was now in the envied position to gain us all state healthcare, so armed with only confidence and naivety we both headed over to our nearest clinic, grabbed a ticket from the deli counter inspired number system and took a seat in line. The Spanish, knowing full well that we Brits as a nation are a lazy bunch, had sourced a couple of bilingual volunteers to sit behind a desk to help with the form filling. Once our number was called we plonked ourselves down in front of these saviours and came face to face with a pretty young local woman and sat beside her, Blanche from the Golden Girls.

"Hello, we are new to the area, and we need some healthcare please" I proclaimed in an over enthusiastic tone.

"Where do you live? Do you own or rent" enquired the elder of the two assistants.

"Ermm… We don't actually have a permanent address as yet, we are staying up a mountain in a wooden shack next to a goat farm but we are hoping to move into Fuengirola centre pretty soon…to escape the Kitty eating vampire slayer" I replied with good humour.

"Do you have an NIE" interrupted the Spanish interpreter without acknowledging my ice breaker.

"My husband has one through his job, I'm going to apply for mine, I promise" I replied nervously.

"Residency? Social Security Number?" I shook my head, sinking further into the chair. My thighs making an unattractive sucking noise as they tried to detach themselves from the plastic seating.

"Then may I suggest you go and get all these items first and then when you've moved into your permanent accommodation, head over to the town hall and register for empadronamiento" smiled the elder assassin through her shiny non government funded white teeth.

With tails firmly between our legs, we reversed out towards the exit, mumbling our thanks and headed into a wall of humid air, clutching our dose of reality like a poor consolation prize.

"Well, that went well" sighed my husband "shall we go and cheer ourselves up with a glass of something cold which doesn't require a prescription?" I nodded my affirmation, trying not to think about all the things we had to do to enable us to claw our way into the Spanish system. **A familiar expat voice cuts through the silence, a departing dart aimed directly towards our retreating bullseye,**

"and don't forget all your British documents need to be apostilled too!!"

Looking up towards the midday sun I sighed and whispered to my spouse,

"Sod the glass, better make it a bottle".

LITTLE HOUSE
ON THE WARY

"**M**um, where's my lunch box? I need clean shorts for PE and I don't want a sandwich today, can I have pasta? Everyone else brings pasta and I've been invited to a party tonight so I need a present and card!"

"Darling, Can you drop me off at the theatre after the school run but I'll need picking up at 4pm to come back home to eat and get changed before returning for tonight's show. Can I also have Pasta for lunch?"

"Woof woof, walk, ball, sniff, wee, sniff sniff ....COCKROACH!! Ahhhhhh!! RUN!! Woof woof ball...ball... yawn... Any pasta left?"

This stimulating conversation can be heard most mornings around 8am high up in the Campo. As I am the only one in the house without a job/school/4 legs I have become the designated driver, taking my passengers into Fuengirola for their daily routine but after the eighth round trip in a 16 hour period I realise as lovely as living in the country is, it's not really conducive to a working life. Or my sanity.

Every sensible piece of advice I have researched online over the last 2 years recommends renting a property for at least a year before deciding what area of Spain to buy your forever home in. Expat forums are full of nightmare neighbour stories and tales of solitude and broken marriages due to choosing the wrong location. Tearing my eyes away from a particular annoying episode of 'Loose Women' I suddenly realise that a) Coleen Nolan may actually be my long lost twin sister and b) I have never listened to anyone's advice in my life.

Making an executive decision from the comfort of the sofa I fire up the lap top and head straight to 'Property for Sale' on Idealista. Cramming a Custard cream into my mouth I hastily type 'Mijas and surrounding areas' into the search bar. With a strong coffee in hand I sit perusing the fantastic villas on offer for the same price as a small country in Eastern Europe and slowly start to whittle my way down from detached Villa, to town house and eventually accept the reality of an apartment which the only viable option if we want to live in the centre of a town where the facilities we require are in abundance. Luckily enough we have already transferred our UK money over to Spain with the help of an exchange company so we have the funds readily available.

I shortlist several properties that look like they have both solid walls and neighbours with teeth and bookmark them ready to show my husband when he returns from his day behind the spotlight. Rather pleased with myself for making this momentous decision without the aid of Vodka or a spouse I load the hairy one into the boot of the car and we head off in high spirits to buy provisions for the week.

Spotting a recently vacated parking space, I reverse the Jeep in-between two scuffed mopeds and languidly wander into Fuengirola town centre with canine in tow. Estate agents fight for dominance along the tree lined street and I press my nose up against the glass frontage, attempting to find the diamond amongst the rough.

"Can I help you?" breathes a voice into my ear and I jump back in surprise, tripping over Brian in the process and after a brief tango with the lead I end up on my knees in front of the stranger in a rather compromising position. Cursing under my breath I drag myself upright and arrive nose to nose with a rather tanned blonde man in a crisp linen suit. Without invitation he kisses me on both cheeks and then just to make sure the introductions are complete, he grasps my hand and pumps it up and down so vigorously I half expect water to start pumping out of my elbow.

"I saw you looking in the window at our wonderful selection of properties and I thought this is a lady who knows what she wants!!" I smile uncertainly and look around for an escape route.

"Would you like to have a look at what properties we have on offer?" I have water for the Perro and chilled wine for the lady!" winks the stranger and flashes his arctic white veneers in my direction.

Caught off guard and slightly light headed from the heat I can feel my resolve beginning to falter. Without further invitation a firm hand is placed in the small of my back and I am ushered over the threshold into the air conditioned den of iniquity.

Plonking myself down onto the white leather sofa I slowly release my grip on reality and rapidly replace it with a chilled glass of wine. My fair haired companion repositions himself behind the Oak desk, strokes down the crease in his trousers and looks me directly in the eye.

"Soooo Senora, what's your budget?"

GAME OF HOMES

"**S**o let me get this right, you went out for a Pomegranate and a pack of digestives and you came back with six bottles of cava and a new apartment???"

Nodding my head in agreement, I smile up at my long suffering wide eyed spouse and offer him another glass of sparkling wine to soften the blow. He looks at me in amazement, shakes his head in disbelief, then downs the chilled fizz in one go.

In all fairness, I haven't actually signed any paperwork or exchanged any of our hard earned cash just yet. I have in fact lined up three properties to view and my husband has to guess which one I've chosen, and if we have both chosen the same one then we buy it. Simple. All the apartments are in (or around) our £120k budget and all are vacant and ready to move into. My other half rubs his pulsating temples and heaves himself out of the safety of the rented sofa, mumbles something about quick divorces and promptly heads towards the shower.

"Don't take long; the agent is picking us up in 20 minutes!!" I yell after him and then turn on my heel and find myself nose to nose with my son.

Tilting his head he looks at me with molten brown questioning eyes "One thing you've failed to mention, does it have a pool and can I walk to school?" He enquires.

I smile at the simplicity of childhood, ruffle his hair and whisper "Get your shoes on and let's go and see!"

A horn beeps outside the gate and we both jump in unison. A loud curse can be heard upstairs and then the sound of running water promptly stops. I smile at my son and clap my hands in childish glee, grabbing my handbag en route to the door while my son shakes his head and waits for the only actual adult in the house to get dry and join us.

Mr. Veneers is stood by the open car door smoking a cigarette and warily eying up the goats who have decided to see who is paying them a visit this balmy evening. Edging closer, I battle my way through the assortment of hairy bodies and hurl myself into the back seat of the air conditioned chariot. A brown nose presses itself up against the window and looks at my straw handbag beseechingly, then bleats at me in apparent longing.

Within minutes all four of us are safely ensconced in the Fiat Panda and heading up the Calahonda hills to view the first of what could be our future home. I smile happily around the car and am met with a steely glare from my still slightly damp other half. The car screeches to a halt in front of a terracotta building and our estate agent leads the way up a stone staircase to the third floor and opens the front door with a flourish. I nod at my husband to enter the property first and he and the boy child step over the threshold.

The apartment is immaculate and fully furnished. With two double bedrooms, a large lounge and dining room and a sun bathed south facing balcony. I brush my hand over the upholstery and look up to see if I can read my husband's expression. His jaw has softened as he takes in the distant sea view.

"Well, what do you think?" I gently enquire "do you like it?"

Nodding his head in my direction he looks me straight in the eye for the first time since arriving and grunts his approval. The boy child has already decided what bedroom he wants if we decide this is the chosen one and also where his computer can go. All the furniture is included in the asking price and the British owners are keen to sell.

With hands on hips our tour guide tells us about the communal swimming pool and the bus times which head into Fuengirola along the A7. I look at my spouse and my son, both like the apartment; I can see it in their faces. It's a readymade home, equipped to move into without any fuss.

Catching the agent's eye he nods in affirmation of my eagerness to move on and leads us all out the front door and back down to the car to view property number two.

Halfway down the external stone stairs the heavens suddenly open and a torrent of rain begins to fall. Laughing at our bad fortune, we all head quickly into the car and jump through the open passenger door. Bemoaning the change in weather I turn to my husband and smile… but he's not there.

I wind down the window and look around for him. The sound of thunder muffles my voice as I call out his name but there is no reply. Shielding my eyes from the deluge I walk back towards the entrance of the block but he is nowhere to be seen. I move my sodden locks away from my face and call out his name again.

A glimpse of blue catches my eye and slowly I turn my head towards the apartment we have just viewed. Floating at the bottom of the stairs like a forlorn rubber fish is one familiar solitary size 10 flip flop minus its owner…

TRADING SPACES

C lutching the solitary flip flop in my hand I tear up the rain soaked stone steps, searching for my husband around every sodden stair. Finally, on hearing a deep groan I turn the last corner to find him lying in a puddle of his own discomfort, sprawled across the floor like the world's most unfortunate incarnation of Cinderella, grasping his swollen ankle and expressing profanities so detailed I refrain from making any Prince charming jokes until his mouth has been washed out with carbolic soap.

"I fell down the bloody stairs and not one of you noticed" he yells up to me through the falling raindrops and then makes a feeble attempt to reintroduce his foot to its runaway soul mate. After several failed attempts he shoves the rubber shoe into his pocket and sits with arms folded, sulking on the tiles.

Trying to stifle an impending giggle I turn away and twiddle with my zipper. I make a mental note to refrain from laughing at people who fall over, even though Harry Hill appears to have made a small fortune from it.

But the harder I try and convince myself to not make light of the situation, the harder my shoulders start to shake and the stupidity of the situation finally overrides any matrimonial compassion and I throw my head back and let out a peal of laughter.

After the giggles have finally tailored off into hiccups, I uncross my legs and hold a tentative hand out to my spouse who promptly brushes my fingers away, hauls himself upright, dusts off his injured pride and hobbles down the steps to join us all in the estate agents car. Mr. Veneers is trying his best to sully his dental investment with several Marlboro lights and the boy child; unaware of the events unfolding around him is tapping his foot in time to whoever happens to be flavour of the month on his iphone.

No one comments along the short journey as to why the Costa del Sol's latest incarnation of Lord Lucan was delayed on level three for such a long time. In all honesty, looking at his petulant face, no one would dare.

The sun evaporates the remaining black clouds as we gallop steadily along the A7 from Calahonda over to our next destination, Mijas Golf. Bleached villas and Orange Blossom adorn the roadside as we climb the whitewashed village, finally stopping in front of a pretty terraced house which overlooks a sparkling communal pool set in stunning surroundings.

Entering the front door we walk/hobble straight into a dining room come kitchen which leads directly out onto a private terrace. Every picture I have seen depicting what we could actually afford in southern Spain is brought to life within this home. It has the two bedrooms we require and also the two bathrooms we will undoubtedly need once the inevitable visitors start arrive and the views are simply stunning. Boy child, already bored in the pursuit of utopia sits out on the sun-drenched balcony and grunts his approval as we point out various landmarks.

I lean upon a potted Palm and breathe in the tranquility. My husband sits on a deck chair and places his hands behind his head, swollen ankle and injured pride all but a distant memory.

"Soooo.....are we ready to move onto our final property of the day?" a voice echoes above my head. I nod in agreement and we reluctantly close the door on what could be our future home.

"This last property is one that has been on the market awhile and been reduced in price for a quick sale. You will either love it or hate it. Are you all ready to go and have a look at something completely different from what we have already seen?" asks our realtor with a smile.

I nod my head in affirmation as my husband crosses his arms in realization while my son stretches his legs in resignation as we head off into the sunset of our final destination.

THE GOOD, THE FAB
AND THE UGLY

"**S**o here we are at the final apartment lined up for today", yells our Commission driven Chauffer as he screeches to a halt and vaults onto the pavement with his front tires. "Granted, it's different from the rest we've viewed, but what it lacks in external beauty and glamour, it makes up for in location. Go and let yourself in, here are the keys, I'm just off to buy some fags"

Standing on the side of the busy road, my husband turns to me in what appears to be a *'Have you finally lost your mind'* sort of way. I wave the keys in the air and cross the road to a small concealed entrance nestling next door to what appears to be a second hand Spanish TV repair shop.

My son removes his headphones and looks up towards our destination

"You are kidding mum... right? We aren't going in here are we? Where's the swimming pool? In fact where's the door?"

Pushing them both aside and tutting at their lack of vision, I open the metal gate and head inside. A spiral stone staircase leads us up to the first floor and after a quick tussle with a sticky lock; I open the door to our final property with a flourish.

Sunshine streams through the south facing windows and onto the speckled marble floor. Stepping straight into the freshly painted white entrance hall the glaringly obvious fact is, there isn't one item of furniture included in the apartment apart from a forlorn looking mattress propped up in the corner of the entrance hall.

"Well that's your bedroom sorted" I yell over my shoulder to the boy child but he's not listening, he's already found the key to the balcony and is currently stood outside.

"Muuuummmm, is that the road leading to my school over there?' he says, pointing behind the trees.

"Why yes, yes it is, what are the odds on that!" I smile innocently. "And look" I exclaim "There's a supermarket on the corner and a Panaderia just to the right. I guess it must only be a ten minute walk down to Miramar, where the English cinema is, you could walk there on your own or with your mates after school, unlike the other two properties which are very pretty but not so central. The sea could be your swimming pool" I smile knowingly and meander back inside.

My husband narrows his eyes at me and I avoid his glare by cheerfully pointing out the space in the remaining vacant rooms.

"There's an extra bedroom here too for when the family want to visit" I cut in before he has time to interject "We could then use this third one as a TV room and put in a sofa bed which would mean we still have a nice quiet dining room where we can all chat and have dinner together like the locals do"

I have it all worked out, an estate agent in the making. Mr. Veneers will be so proud of his protégé.

Begrudgingly my husband raps his knuckles against the kitchen wall and looks enquiringly into lounge. I can see what he's thinking. Knock the kitchen wall through; bring the kitchen into the dining room. I thought exactly the same when I first viewed the property. I clench my sweating palms together, willing him to see the potential of this empty shell.

A voice echoes out from the balcony where my only child is still standing, leaning over the railings.

"So let me get this right, if we lived here I could get up for school about 8.15am and walk over the road on my own, meet my friends at the weekends and I wouldn't need to be seen out in public with either of you two ever again?"

I nod my head in agreement and then look at my husband and aim my final arrow at the standing target

"And just so you know, the theatre is just a ten minute walk away but I thought you could buy that motorbike you always wanted…and ride that to work, then we could get rid of the car which would solve the parking issue"

Casually I walk back into the lounge and leave the men folk looking slightly shell shocked on the balcony, the realization of my words finally taking effect.

The front door gently opens and the Porcelain Prince glides into the room and stands quietly beside me.

"Soooo… have you done my job for me?" he whispers into my ear.

Looking out onto the balcony I watch my husband and son talking animatedly and pointing up the road towards the town centre whilst laughing at the mopeds flying past on the road below.

My lips curve into a smile and I nod towards the 'Se Vende' sign hanging lopsided from the outside railings. Nodding, He makes a scissoring motion with his fingers and rubs his hands in glee.

My work here is done.

PACK TO THE FUTURE

"**A**nd how would you like to pay the property deposit Senora?"

The reality of our purchase is finally starting to sink in and I can feel my palms getting clammy as we all sit in silence signing the Spanish legal documents. I could be selling the family kidneys for all I can understand but we sign our joint names on the dotted line and then everyone in the office shakes hands in universal agreement. We enlisted the help of a monetary transfer company who moved the proceeds seamlessly from one account to another so that's one thing less we have to worry about. Before you can say 'I've changed my mind, I'll spend that £10k in Puerto Banus on a pair pneumatic breasts instead' the money is already in the grasping hands of the solicitors and the deeds are being drawn up.

Sitting afterwards on the wall outside the lawyer's lair, the mid afternoon sun beating upon our weary heads, I suddenly realise that within a month we could be in our own home. We will be mortgage free for the first time in our lives. Granted, we will only have 53p left in our bank account to live on but you can't expect to be a home owner AND afford to eat.

"So what happens now?" asks a bewildered husband. "Do we buy furniture? We gave all of ours away in the UK. This must be the only unfurnished property for sale in the whole of the Costa Del Sol!"

I scratch my head. I hadn't actually thought this far ahead. I'd spent the last 36 months watching relocation programmes and planning our escape from Brexit, not looking in IKEA catalogues.

"And, now you know where we are going to be living, you can get a job" breathes my spouse into my ear "No excuses now!" He smiles (rather maliciously may I add) and saunters off to purchase a coffee.

Little does he know that I have already got an interview lined up for the following day. Granted, it's a commission only position but really, how difficult can selling sun cream around various hotel pools actually be? This time next year I'll be the same colour as David Dickenson and I'll be paid for the privilege. Picking up my handbag I make my way over to the jeep and we all head back over the rugged roads in good spirits to our temporary house in the campo.

Brian the brave is the first to vault out of the car and I suddenly realise that we won't have the luxury of a garden anymore. No more letting him out to wee at 8am. I'll have to get dressed and walk him, come rain or shine. He'd grown quite accustomed to the local goats and headless kittens surrounding the grounds and just last night he had appeared at the front door slightly delirious after his evenings ablutions, eyes rotating with some strange and pungent foliage attached to the side of his mouth, a canine version of 'Bez' from the Happy Mondays. It took almost an hour to coach him off the shed roof after attempting, rather unsuccessfully to fly alongside the fruit bats.

Entering the house, I go to put the kettle on and lean up against the cooker and stare at our worldly possessions lying in a discarded mound in the corner of the dining room. All our pots and pans and furniture had been given away to family and friends and what stood before me was just a jumble of memories of our former life awaiting its final resting place in a small apartment in Fuengirola. Tears pricked the back of my eyes as the weight of my decision rested heavily on my shoulders.

"Erm,.. Mum, there's a woman walking up the gravel drive dragging a very large backpack and shouting your name and waving a bottle of wine at me..?"

Turning on my heel I squint out the window to see a very real ghost of my nomadic and hedonistic past walking confidently into our present and, no doubt about to change our imminent future.

TO THE MANOR BURN

"**W**hat the hell are you doing here, and more importantly, how on Google earth did you find us?"

I smile and grasp my nomadic friend to my breast and breathe in the heady scent of her travels. Memories as ripe as a week old nectarine flood into my head and I'm instantly transported back to 1994...

...I'm age 27 and on a one way flight to Hong Kong. I have no money, nowhere to stay and no idea what I am going to do once I arrive. I blame Judith Charmers. It was after a particularly horrendous shift working in Harrods (home to the obscenely rich and rigorously rude) the platinum blonde Irish presenter did a feature on us Brits working side by side in this affluent Asian city and suddenly, all thoughts of attending drama school become nothing but a distant memory. Without rhyme or reason nor a week's working notice, I packed up my troubles, purchased a one way ticket and spent the following 2 years of my young life living, laughing, surviving and residing on the 16th floor of the notorious Chunking Mansions alongside a series of other misfit Gweilo expats. Working till dawn in Chinese karaoke bars to pay for our adventures and then wiping sleep out of our eyes at 5am to appear as extra's alongside Jackie Chan in his latest action movie. Life was good, life was exciting, life was...

"How did you find me?" I laugh between hugs "I can't even find me living out here??"

"I was up in the Andalucía Mountains and I saw on Face book that you had moved to Spain so I thought I'd pop in and see you. That Goat farmer across the road was really helpful, pointed me in the right direction and even offered me some fresh milk!" My old acquaintance informs me with a smile a she wipes away the residue on her lips.

Dropping her rucksack onto the wooden floor and stretching out her aching spine, introductions are made and edited adventures are told. As the final bottle of wine is emptied my newest housemate, of which normality was never an option yawns and closes her well travelled eyes.

Leading her up to the largest of spare rooms to sleep off the most recent of travels I close the door quietly behind me and make my way back into the lounge where my husband is sitting with an open laptop in front of him

"Why didn't you say you had an interview tomorrow?" He asks in a sullen tone

"Because if I don't take the job then you won't be any the wiser" I reply, almost shutting his fingers between the lid in my haste to close the incriminating email down.

He harrumphs his disagreement and I march off to bed alone with laptop in hand.

The morning is greeted with the usual array of animal activity, culminating in a sparrow flying through the bedroom window and crapping on the duvet before seeking solace behind the wardrobe. My husband sleeps through the whole arm waving and bird poking adventure so I leave man and feathered friend alone to get better acquainted.

Leaving our guest to sleep off her adventures, I make my way downstairs and steal the jeep before anyone says they need running anywhere. With the wind in my hair and Ricky Martin bellowing in my ear, I make my way to the hotel where I am to be educated on how to correctly apply sun cream and charm the tourists into buying my wares.

In all honesty, I don't know how flogging specialised lotion could possibly be classed as a 'job' but with a spring in my stride I walk into the foyer to be immediately greeted by a very slim, perma tanned middle aged woman who instantly has me sign 39 forms on product confidentiality and then strides outside into the pool area to show me how to flog creams to bronzed sitting ducks.

Within 30 minutes I know without hesitation the job is not for me. Firstly, having to get down on bended knee to talk to customers is not boding well with my clacking joints. Every time I try to rise I have the grip the sun lounger with such force I almost propel one baking punter into the pool along with his half consumed pinacolada. Secondly, the amount of spiel you are required to impart to the reluctant purchaser about skin damage makes me seriously wonder about my mahogany companion's skin care routine and thirdly, when you are not flogging your creams and sprays, you have to stand in the sun, never in the shade to prove how well the product works!

Being the well adjusted, mature middle aged responsible woman I am, I cross my legs and make my excuses, head towards the toilet, veer swift left and make a bid for freedom out the front door and onto the street. Swinging my bag over my shoulder I head towards the car, picking up a bottle of fizzy wine en route.

Becoming an adult with a job can wait until tomorrow.

THE FLIRTY DOZEN

On the car journey back to our borrowed house in the Campo, I had time to reflect on what we had learned (and achieved) in our first few weeks of being in sunny Spain...

1: The second hand Jeep we spontaneously purchased in the same time it takes to consume several strips of the Colonels secret recipe had completed the full 1,374 mile trip from Hastings to Mijas without as much as a splutter with husband, hound and the complete works of Stephen King encased in its padded compound.

2: The menopausal woman and 'don't talk to me in public' actually navigated their way via plane, train and automobile up into the Mijas hills and locate Heidi's hidden house without the aid of nicotine, Google Maps, Valium or Vodka.

3: All four founding members of the 'sod it lets go to Spain' brigade were reunited within 30 hours of leaving the sanctity of Sussex and didn't encounter one placard saying 'turn back now you bunch of Brexiteering loonies' (we voted remain, obviously).

4: Brian is now afraid of kittens, with or without their heads attached and now truly believes he is part goat. He can be found most mornings bleating at passing cars from his favourite view point on top of the corrugated shed.

5: Everyone survived drinking the Spanish tap water after hopping from foot to foot in the kitchen for 30 minutes going "you drink it, no YOU drink it". Wine was not really a valid option just before the school run.

6: If you are foolish enough to forget that the Spaniards enjoy a day off from hurling your edible goods down a stationary conveyer belt you may, as I did, arrive at Mercadona on a Sunday morning and stand sleepily in front of the automatic door for a good 30 minutes until realizing that shops actually close one day a week in Spain. In all honesty you can survive the weekend without replenishing your digestives and go out for a nice lunch instead.

7: Numerous children roam the unlit side roads into the early hours and bolt about on scooters and bikes and give each other 'backies' down crowded pavements. Play Stations are just something they construct out of cardboard in abandoned houses.

8: There are jobs here in Spain; you just have to look for them. If you are fortunate enough to get one with a contract you will be automatically entitled to healthcare as long as you don't mind filling in 17,000 forms and sending your various birth and marriage certificates back to their place of origin to be verified and translated. Our most recent lot of paperwork has had a lovely vacation in Vegas and came back with a stunning tan.

9: Moving house is stressful enough but relocating to a country where the only thing you can pronounce correctly is 'hello', even more so. Get everything in order before you leave home and be prepared to stand in various queues. There is a 50/50 chance you may reach the front of the line at some point before the shutter is slammed down for the night. A three hour siesta in Spain is classed as a 'a short break'.

10: A drinkable Rioja is sometimes cheaper to purchase in the supermarket than a bottle of water.

11: You will demand a divorce from your spouse on a number of occasions while attempting to get your solicitor to call you back to see if the sale on your desired property is progressing before Brexit occurs. If I had a Euro for every time my husband yelled "you wanted to move here!" I would have enough money to purchase a family friendly hit man to bump him off and have enough left over to get a widows tummy tuck afterwards.

12: Hearing your child conversing in Spanish to his school mates will make you prouder than winning the mum's egg and spoon race. Waking up to the sun streaming in through the window and not having to take out a second mortgage to dine out is exhilarating. Knowing that all the people back in the UK who sucked air through their teeth when you said you were moving 'away' are still sat at home on a cold December evening while you are on the beach having a BBQ with all your new nomadic comrades.

BREAKING BED

"I told you it was too big! The first time I laid eyes on it I said it wouldn't fit up that tiny gap and now it's well and truly stuck. You'll have to find another suitable entrance to shove it in if you're determined to get it up!"

Storming back up to the apartment I leave my husband and two very confused Spanish delivery men encased on the communal spiral staircase lodged behind one very obstinate king sized mattress. Slamming the door behind me I wipe the sweat off my menopausal brow and pick up a copy of the local Olive Press newspaper and fan myself back into some semblance of sanity.

Within 4 weeks of saying 'I do' to our little Fuengirola flat, papers had been signed, hands had been shaken and just 18 hours earlier the majority of the profit from our Hastings home had been handed over to three squabbling siblings in exchange for a set of rusty keys. And now, before we can finally settle in to our new life in the Sun, we have to find something to sleep on, and that something is nestling quite comfortably half way up the shady staircase of our hastily purchased first floor abode.

"Paula, stop moping and get your arse out onto the balcony, we have a plan B!" yells a familiar voice from outside. Hauling said posterior off the marble floor I peer over the railings and see two tanned plus one beetroot face looking expectantly up at me.

"Apparently, they are going to wrap a rope around it and I'm going to haul it over the balcony, well I think that's what they said...either that or they are going to hang me so PLEASE open the door and let me in!"

Reluctantly I press the buzzer, mumbling profanities to the silent walls and within moments 'he who knows best' puffs past me and heads out onto the sunny terrace.

Five minutes later a makeshift pulley has been attached to the railings and my husband stands precariously on the wrong side of the balcony facing the busy road. One hand grips the wrought iron balustrade and the other a piece of cord which is attached to a very large and cumbersome mattress.

"Don't drop it" I yell helpfully as sweat drips off his 'verging on fifty' fore-head. The two delivery men, no doubt used to stupid foreigners purchasing products too big for their rose tinted abodes, haul the bed above their heads and start the countdown. My husband, tethered to the railings by his Dunelm dressing gown cord, leans precariously over the edge, nervously facing the pavement and grabs the hem of the polythene cover with the tip of his fingers. Without further instruction, the younger of the two Spanish workers vaults onto his partners shoulders and gives the mattress a final shove and husband, bed and common sense fall backwards over the balcony railings, landing together in an ungainly heap upon the terracotta floor.

Brian (the brave) having watched all this from the comfort of a canopied shady corner, meanders over to see what is occurring and having found not one solitary digestive crumb en route, circles the area a couple of times before settling himself on the mattress which is currently residing on top of my motionless husband. Shoving the disgruntled hound off his coveted new bed, I grasp my spouse's barely visible hand and haul him out from under his plastic prison and between us gently lay the troublesome slumber down up against the apartment wall. Delivery forms are finally signed and the other less cumbersome objects are placed in the rooms they were duly purchased for.

"Well, that's good, we finally have something to sit on, something to sleep on, and something to eat off and oh, something odd to look at until the Telly arrives!". My husband's eyes dart warily over to the cobalt black, four foot glass mosaic face I hastily purchased after several glasses of Andalucía's finest homegrown. I glare at him from the comfort of our new sofa bed

51

and ignore his last remark.

Looking around the white washed walls , an empty shell full of possibilities, the truth hits home and I realise I will never, ever have to mow a wet lawn in November again. No mortgage, no biting winters, no more poundland....no more...

A thought suddenly strikes me and it chills me to the core, what properties am I going to covet now whilst watching channel 4???

ABSOLUTELY FAGULOUS

"**M**um, why won't my Xbox work?" Bellows a frustrated voice from behind his bedroom door.

"We don't have any internet" I sigh, and unpack yet another box. "WHAT???? How can I survive?? I can't talk to anyone! Even the goat house had internet, what am I supposed to do???"

"Get off your arse and go outside and chat to real people?" I mumble to myself and place a family picture against the wall to be mounted when 'Lighting Guy' returns from flattering the luvvies in sepia. Our worldly possessions had finally arrived intact the day before, delivered by a very nice man with a very big van. Looking now at the mountain of boxes stacked against the walls I realise that I haven't packed one kitchen utensil, not even a side plate or a fork. But we had, in our wisdom, brought along the 4 foot long fiberglass sharks head which is currently residing on the balcony underneath the washing line. Foolishly I had been under the assumption that every fleeing expat with a property to sell in Spain would leave their abode fully furnished, like a Wimpy show home from the 1980's. But we purchased from locals, and locals take everything with them, including the shower head apparently.

To add insult to injury we also have no hot water. The ancient gas boiler didn't even make an attempt to fire up. It just stood there, white and lackluster, mocking my sweaty armpits with silent insolence. I wander back through the kitchen, trying to avoid eye contact with the ramshackle lime green Formica units. I half expect Miss Jones to come wandering around the corner at any given moment asking where Rigsby is lurking. Standing forlornly with my head pressed against the dining room wall, I try to calm the panic that I can feel, once again, bubbling inside of me.

Standing up straight and brushing Brian's dog hair off my leggings, I look at the clock. It's barely 10am on a Saturday morning but without any wardrobes to place our clothes in, the outside world looks far more appealing than my current enclosure. Dragging the petulant one out of his bed, we amble over to Miramar shopping centre and stand in line at the Moviestar desk, waiting patiently to speak to the solitary staff member who speaks English, hoping he can enable our access back into the 21st century without the need of a Tardis.

Two hours later we claim possession of a ridiculously extortionate phone contract with the promise that fibre optic will be installed 'directly' into our flat forthwith.

The midday sun beats down upon scantily clad tourists and we decide to take a pitstop to fill our growling bellies at a local café. My son orders enough food to feed a small army and I pick at his leftovers whilst clutching a chilled white wine, my personal buoyancy aid amid a sea of uncertainty.

Sitting at the table opposite me is a blonde woman of similar age who is talking rapidly into her mobile phone in French and flicking cigarette ash onto the pavement. She catches my eye and smiles, raising her eyebrows in a conspiratorial 'are people actually this stupid' motion and slams her phone onto the table and inhales another round of nicotine. Her brown eyes swivel in my direction and land directly on my rapidly evaporating glass of wine.

"I think I'll join you in one of those" she says in perfect clipped English tones and waves the waiter over. "Would you like another?" she enquires then orders two white wines before I have time to decline her generous offer.

Devoid of any real adult conversation since moving into our new home, I motion for her to join us at the table and my son, full of tapas and fresh Naranja, makes his excuses and ambles back towards the direction of the flat, no doubt to see if the god of fibre optic communication has miraculously embedded itself into our walls.

"Soooo" my new platinum friend enquires with a wave of her hand, wafting a plume of smoke in my direction "What do the people with children do here in the summer months? My 2 boys don't start school for another 12 weeks, we've literally just moved over here from France and they need to find some form of activity apart from exercising their wrists on the Xbox...."

I smile and lean forward in my plastic chair, fuelled by lack of carbs and too much cheap wine. The person sitting accross from me is a complete stranger but I hear my voice engage before my brain has time to complain.

"I'm also a new wife in the sun, and I think I may have an idea....'

SAVING PRIVATE BRIAN

"**B**oot Camp? Like in the Military? I don't even own any boots, only trainers. Is Brian going too?"

My son stares at me through narrowed eyes, arms crossed, already a couple of inches above me in height and leagues ahead of me in attitude. Prepared for his reaction, I silently place a flyer in front of him which explains the 5 day summer course based up in the Alhaurin hills called '**Eagles Training Camp**'. With a sullen expression he reads it, grunts a couple of times and then looks back up at me.

"So, basically it's like the scouts but with no dib dibbing, considerably hotter with mutant sized mosquitoes?" an eyebrow is raised enquiringly.

I nod my head in agreement and remain quiet as he takes the pamphlet into his bedroom and closes the door. I can hear the familiar sound of the X box controller being taken out of its stand and I reach for the phone, hoping he will forgive me in years to come for making this decision on his behalf.

Thinking back to my own childhood filled with fresh air and

conkers amid endless summer holidays, I smile at the recollection of my bygone youth. San izal, a prerequisite in every 70's school toilet, no Labrador puppies in those days I can tell you. Then once we escaped the confines of our dusty classrooms, playing kiss chase until the sun set over our freckled faces. Faggots and peas or Findus crispy pancakes graced most of the dinner tables in our cul de sac, in fact anything highly processed and on offer at Kwik Save being the staple diet of most children of the 70's, the more E numbers, the better.

Looking down at my weathered hands, I dial the number on the flyer and after a brief conversation with a lovely lady called Debbie, the wife of Mickey (ex military, no nonsense, bog hands) my only child is booked on the 5 day survival course which provides children & teens the basic skills to cope in the wilderness, and also how to deal with bullies in the real world. The small selection of boys and girls would sleep in adjoining tents placed adjacent to the family house, high up in the hills and I smile to myself, wishing I was young again and able to happily function on a daily basis without the aid of HRT or Silverkrin.

Sitting on our apartment balcony I hold the still warm phone in my hand and look out over the street. The world is passing by in a sunny haze of garbled conversation and noisy mopeds. My son's bedroom door opens and he walks over to where I am sat. Silently, he places his arms around my neck and gives me a hug. I smile up into his brown eyes, knowing full well the difficulties he faces, an English child in a foreign land approaching his teenage years.

"Ok, I'll do it, it actually looks good fun. But I want to take lots of Haribo for snacks and get my hair cut before I go". Nodding my head in agreement I hug him back and fail to mention that he is already enrolled starting the following Monday and that, although the camp is in the wilderness, they conveniently have a tuck shop available on site from 3-5pm.

Brian places a paw upon my lap and looks beseechingly at me; it's time for his morning walk. Clipping his lead on, I bribe the boy child to accompany us on our jaunt with the promise of an ice cream en route. The hairy hound is also partial to a lick of a strawberry mivi and we all set off before the sun has time to heat up the pavement below his naked pads.

"Where's the car parked mum? I've not been in it for weeks" my son enquires, as we make our way over the Miramar Bridge. I point in the direction of the car park where our dusty jeep sits forlornly in the corner, patiently awaiting its next adventure.

Unfortunately, the one down side of living in the town centre is the lack of parking. Food shopping is nigh impossible. A trip to Lidl involves double parking outside the apartment, hurling all of the shopping into the communal hall, jumping back into the car, parking it several miles away, sprinting back on foot to the flat to find everything has already defrosted and henceforth, that evenings tea will consist of a various assortment of food items that cannot be refrozen.

"Why don't you sell the car mum and get a couple of motor-bikes; at least we can leave those parked outside the flat...can I have 3 scoops?" he asks all in one breath while perusing the assortment of sugar laden Helado's on offer.

I stop dead in my tracks, of course, this is the obvious solution, why didn't I think of it myself. Flog the car and get a couple of mopeds, do as the locals do, when in Rome and all that. After all, what could possibly go wrong?

WHERE EAGLES SCARE

"**I**ts 0800 hours, rise and shine soldier, these pots won't wash themselves!" I yell into the new recruit's bedroom.

My son opens one eye, looks at me, sighs, turns over and pulls the duvet up over his ears.

"Can't you stay at home mum and let dad take me to boot camp, you're beyond embarrassing" he mumbles from underneath the bedding.

"What, and miss your grand entrance into independence? Not on your Nelly" I reply with a sardonic smile.

Gingerly retracing my steps over the mountain of dirty clothes strewn across the floor, I noisily close the bedroom door behind me and try and ignore the 'where's my socks/hoody/trainers!' dialogue that follows me around the apartment for the next hour.

Once said items have been located (dirty and crumpled in the bottom of the wardrobe as usual) the whole family including

Brian 'the brave' pile into the jeep and head up towards the Al-haurin mountains. The temperature gauge at 9.30am is already heading into the 30's as the summer sunshine beats relentlessly onto the singed Spanish countryside. Boy child brushes his hands over his newly shaven locks and stares out of the window. Brian attempts to consume an old Twix wrapper and my husband hangs one lanky tanned arm out of the window while its white twin hangs forlornly inside the moving vehicle.

"I still can't get used to the fact that the theatre closes down for over two months in the summer" the older of the males says to no one in particular. I nod my head in agreement. Only 3 months into the position of lighting technician and already he has 2 months off. Mentally I compile a list of things that need repairing around the flat, and that list increases steadily by the day. Unfortunately the only room in our humble abode that currently has an air conditioning unit is the lounge so it's akin to entering the Sahara desert when you have to leave the comfort of the chilled room and make your way begrudgingly to bed. The first few hours of attempting sleep is usually spent on top of the sheets mumbling 'it's too hot, are you hot? I'm really hot, get your leg away from me it's too hot'. Of course I hold the 'I'm WAY hotter than you' card, being age 51 and attached permanently to what appears to be an internal furnace with a broken thermostat.

After 17 wrong turns we finally arrive at the camp meeting point and a young lad on a push bike leads the way up to the area which is going to be home to my son for the next 5 days.

"You can drop me off here" boy child mumbles and makes a hasty exit from the confines of the stifling car. Half a dozen teens are loitering around a large green tent listening intently while a man dressed in Khaki shouts out orders. Spotting his latest recruit ambling towards the camp the Commando yells out towards my son "You look tired boy, no doubt up to god knows what time on the Xbox, well there's none of that computerised crap here, pick a bunk and fall into line"

My son, who never does what he's told without argument,

breaks into a sprint, drops his bag onto an empty mattress, places his shoulders upright and joins the other inmates without complaint

"I'm putting in a request for one of those at home" I mumble to my slack jawed husband, pointing at the confident man barking orders at the motley assortment standing before him.

After waving our goodbye's we head back to civilisation in the car and I decided to broach the subject of selling our 4 wheel drive and replacing it with a couple of scooters.

"You can have a scooter, I'm having a 125" my spouse harrumphs then proceeds to make motorbike noises all the way back into civilisation.

I shake my head at the man beside me and smile to myself. It's been a rollercoaster of a journey. In the 4 months we have been living in the Costa del Sol we have bought a property, got our son into school, submitted the mountains of paperwork to enable us to get healthcare and rescued our faithful hound from an attack of the Zombie Pussies.

Staring out the window an idea begins to form. What if I was to write all about our relocation, would anyone actually read about the adventures of a new wife in the sun??

MUCH ADO ABOUT BLOGGING

I'm sat in front of the silent laptop, fingers hovering expectantly over the keys, willing the phrases I use so freely on a daily basis to transport themselves from body to technology. I promised myself I'd write a witty account of our relocation but unfortunately, my aging grey matter has other ideas.

I close my eyes, trying to recall how it felt as we took our first steps into our New life in the Sun all those months ago. I rub my forehead and look out towards the mountains through the window, seeking divine inspiration from my elasticated smalls which are currently wafting themselves dry on a hastily erected rotary line, but they offer no words of wisdom, not even an opening pun. I sigh and get up of my seat. I may as well bring the washing in while awaiting the cascade of witty one liner's to take up residence in my currently uninhabited brain.

Letting myself out onto the balcony I kick an unidentifiable chewed dog toy along the tiles for 'Brian the brave' who hurls himself along the slippery surface, performing a skater's turn before his head makes contact with the back wall. I pick up a couple of dead leaves from a potted plant and then saunter back indoors to the welcoming glare of the empty computer screen. A clap of thunder echoes overhead. I catch a glimpse of several T shirts still waving at me on the line and let out an audible sigh. How the hell I am going to recreate our adventures onto Spanish soil from over four months ago if I can't even remember to bring in my clean cottons when I'm standing right in front of them!

Slamming the laptop lid resolutely shut I get up and mumble profanities all the way to the biscuit tin and consume several sponge fingers before I've even made it to the comfort of the sofa. Brian does his best Paul McKenna death stare, willing the sugary treats to fall in his direction while shadowing me from room to room.

"If I give you a digestive will you go and write my book for me?" I enquire to the salivating hound but the canine one is too busy drowning in his own expectant dribble to adhere to my pleas.

My husband ambles into the lounge, scratching his early morning shadow while simultaneously breaking wind, takes one look at my thunderous expression and crumb laden torso and promptly leaves the room again. "Don't forget you have that audition today for KES at the theatre at 3pm" he yells from the safety of the kitchen "You'll be good in that role, the mother in that is a right misery, you can do some method acting!"

Within two hours I am transformed from Ena Sharples into Ivy Tilsley with makeup and hairspray applied and kitten heels adorned. Standing outside the theatre bar I feel a nervous flutter of excitement, armed only with the prospect of standing on an unfamiliar stage with just a script and my ego to hand.

People of all ages are milling around tables, comparing characters and perfecting Yorkshire accents. I sit on the outskirts watching the women my own age chat good naturedly to each other before their name is called and they head towards the stage, the heavy doors closing behind them, their rendition of this Northern classic to be heard only by the directors in charge.

I toy with the idea of having a swift vodka beforehand to calm my nerves but then decide 'Karaoke Kes' may not be what they are looking for. I see a few familiar faces sat on the table opposite and smile uncertainly in their direction, but I am not invited into the inner sanctum, I have as yet to earn my stripes, I look down at the script before me and mumble random lines into my diet coke.

"Paula Lesk....lesch...lasch....skovitz?" I lift my hand uncertainly and rise from my seat and head towards the Theatre doors. An elderly lady places a number on my blouse and I look down. Number 13, just my sodding luck.

Straightening my shoulders and fluffing up my hair I place a nervous hand onto the velvet clad door and enter the unknown.

Two men are sat waiting by the stage, hands outstretched and smiles adorning their confident faces.

"Ah, I take it you are lighting guys wife, we've heard all about you" they laugh conspiratorially.

Taking a deep breath I look them directly in the eye and in my best Yorkshire accent reply

"Yeah, I bet you bloody ave!"

THE HAM THAT ROCKS THE FABLE

T en minutes later I gently close the auditorium doors behind me and stroll back out into the afternoon sunshine. Several expectant faces look up from their scripts
in anticipation of their name being called to head into the inner
sanctum.

"How did it go?" a female voice makes me jump. A striking bru-
nette, slightly older than me is stood with a glass of wine in her
hand. Dimples form in her cheeks and she motions for me to
join her at the table.

"OK, I think?' and smile, pleased that I may finally have a drinking companion and order myself a glass of white wine and sit
down beside her.

"Have you done any plays previously here at the Theatre?" I
politely enquire and take a sip of my chilled confidence booster.
She shakes her head and a slight frown forms across her smooth
brow "Almost, but not quite…"

Before I can ask what that sentence means her glass clinks
against mine and she leans forwards, dimples in place once

again 'May the best Mrs Casper win' and winks in my direction, and I smile at her good natured camaraderie, only slightly marred by the fact that we are in reality, hoping that the other ones acting skills are, in essence, crap.

"How did it go?" my husband enquires as I saunter back into the apartment a couple of hours later, slightly rosy cheeked and tipsy, tottering uncertainly on my kitten heels. He pauses, cheese toastie half way to his mouth and shakes his head. He knows me too well. I love auditions. The adrenalin, the unknown, the fact that I have only one chance to make a first impression, waiting for the phone to ring, if it rings at all... It's like being a teenager all over again, minus the acne and love bites.

"OK I think?" and then my phone rings... caller unknown.

Grabbing it I put it onto speaker and motion for my husband to be quiet.

Before I've even had time to perfect my Judy Dench inspired acceptance speech a familiar voice echoes down the line.

"Mum, it's me, I'm absolutely knackered, I'm on their phone, I've lost my charger, we've been camping in the woods the last 2 nights, almost got eaten by a wild boar, Then we went swimming in the lake in our undies, anyway, the course has finished, can I have a penknife now? Come and get me and bring a KFC, I'm famished, bye!!"

Without having uttered one solitary word I replace the phone back on the table. Looking towards Brian I shrug my shoulders and he replies with a wag of his tail anticipating a tennis ball appearing from behind my ear or failing that, a digestive from up my sleeve.

Heading out into the evening sun we spend 15 minutes trying to remember where we parked the Jeep then the following 30 minutes trying to get the vehicle started. The engine is as flat as a supermodels chest and I can feel the first sign of panic starting to set in, imagining my son, patience not being one of his virtues, foraging in the forest in search of the lesser spotted chicken dipper. Finally, we manage to flag someone down with a set of jump leads and the neglected engine finally roars into life. Looking beside me I notice Brian has found a disregarded packet of monster munch and is currently sporting a pickled onion flavoured food bag on his snout. Kneeling down I pull the crisp wrapper off his face and shove him into the car. Sweat trickles down my back and I my stomach grumbles in protest at its lack of contents. A phone suddenly starts to ring. My bag is jammed under the car seat and as I pull it out, the contents go flying around the jeeps interior, all apart from my favourite lip gloss which makes its escape out the open window, seeking a new life in the Alhaurin countryside.

The phone goes silent then immediately starts to ring again and I grab it, knowing full well it will be my son asking why he hasn't been picked up yet. Wiping the sweat of my brow I press the answer button

"Hold on, we're bloody coming, your dads got a flat battery and Brians snorted that much MSG his eyes are rotating faster than a fairground Waltzer. Have you had a wash at all this week or am I going to have to hose you down before you step foot back into civilisation...?"

Pausing for breath I wait for my sons reply but an all too familiar theatrical male voice finally cuts through the silence instead "I take it that's a yes then to playing Mrs Casper?"

A MOTHER DAY
IN PARADISE

'Hello Ladies, congratulations on all your auditions, they were all excellent. You'll be pleased to hear that none of you are actually playing the part of the Kestrel, hahahhaaaa'

We all smile politely at the director whilst snatching glances around the room at the other cast members sitting expectantly around the table. I catch the eye of my dimpled friend from the previous week and she gives me a knowing wink.

"The reason we are here today is to have a brief read though of all your roles and to get the feel of the play. Shall we start with introducing ourselves and which character we are playing?"

A blonde lady with a West Country accent starts us off and we rotate round the table. Library assistant, farmer, delivery person and finally it's my turn to speak up. I clear my throat and look up at the expectant faces.

"Hi I'm Paula, I'm new to the theatre and I'm playing Mrs Casper" I smile and raise my palm in an uncertain wave. I look around the table and see a few surprised expressions, so I swiftly return my misplaced greeting into my lap where it rests like a bird without wings.

"Fabulous!" Booms the director ' let's get cracking!'

An elbow nudges me in the ribs. I turn to my left and a voice whispers in my ear "I went for that role". I nod my head solemnly and stay staring at my script, afraid to meet the eyes attached to the voice. I'm fully aware from previous experience that 'Woman in Shop' doesn't really compensate when you've auditioned for a principle role, so I clear my throat and keep my ego and opinion in close check.

A couple of hours and several accents later we are released from the confines of the dusty theatre and I quickly make my excuses and head back out into the sun. Ambling through the streets of old town Fuengirola I raise my face toward the mid summer heat and breathe in the heavy scent of freedom. I still can't quite believe that we own outright our little apartment in this bustling, non apologetic seaside resort and within ten minutes my key is rattling in the front door and I wearily let myself back into our own private corner of utopia.

"I've sold it!" yells my husband as I walk indoors and I know instantly that the Xenia, our little warrior princess of a jeep is no more. Sitting side by side on the balcony we sip a glass of wine and chat about our next mode of transport.

My son, only recently released from the wilderness ambles out onto the terrace and plonks himself on the sofa next to us. I can still smell the mud caked into his pores but his eyes are clear with excitement.

"So, as it was my idea, can I have a moped too?" he looks at us in anticipation, already revving the engine with his mind's eye.

"No you can't!" I reply in no uncertain terms "but you can help us choose which one you fancy sitting on the back off...your dad is getting a 125, less embarrassing apparently than a twist and go" I say winking in my husband's direction.

With reluctance my 'I'm almost a teenager' accepts his passenger status and all three of us look online at shiny vehicles with two wheels as opposed to our usual four. Within the hour we have contacted a local chap who deals in second hand bikes who is prepared to bring a couple over so we can have a test drive the following morning.

And so without drama, we all sit companionably together and watch the sun set over the Andalucía Mountains, laughing at the adventures which have already occurred and eagerly awaiting the ones that are yet to arrive.

CARELESS VESPA

"**I**'ve decided to forego my soul and become an estate agent"

My husband, a man used to my vast array of career choices just nods his head and continues to eat his Spanish Allbran

"I'm serious, a friend of a friends husband is working as one and he says you don't need any qualifications and it's the easiest way to make decent money along the coast and he's prepared to train me up. I'm starting tomorrow"

I finally pause for breath and await his approval.

"Go for it Hoogstraten, I'm more than happy to become a kept man. Is there any more milk in the fridge?"

I shouldn't be surprised by his reply. I have had a fair few careers since I left school in 1984. Over a 100 at the last count. My husband has had two. Most people count sheep when they go to bed, I count the numerous opportunities that have been handed to me. The trouble is, I love a good interview, I just don't usually like the actual job. I'm sure I have ADHD.

My first foray into gainful employment was a season as 'Henry the Happy Howler' in Pontins, Blackpool. That job was short lived as I overheated on the first Summers day whilst clad in the orange dog suit, passing out on top of a small child currently having his photo taken with my alter ego.

Then as an only child I suddenly decided I wanted to care for others people's offspring and not just crush them so I promptly took a position as a nanny for three small kids aged one, three and five. If I'm honest, the main reason I wanted the role was because it was based in Israel and after a brief stint as a hairdresser I wanted to see much more than just the inside of a pensioners beehive. Unfortunately on arriving in Tel Aviv, I realised my teenage self didn't actually like the fruit of others peoples loins or the reality of working a 15 hour day, or working at all if I'm honest...

Anyway, I digress. I was now going to make a fortune selling property and purchase me some Botox and a bit of liposuction with my first proper Spanish pay cheque.

Staring at the contents of my wardrobe I realised that anything resembling office wear had a size 12 label in the collar and I was currently verging on a stout 16. Slamming the offending closet door closed I consoled myself with a ham sandwich and promised to cut out carbs starting from tomorrow.

The sound of rainfall dripping onto the air conditioning unit dragged me from my slumber the following morning and I forced my ever expanding hips into a pair of 'all you can eat' leggings and a borrowed blouse. By 9am I was ready to make my first million and headed outside to straddle my latest mode of transport, a second hand blue Vespa purchased only a few days earlier which sat alongside my husband's larger bike.

Staring down at the wet seat I suddenly realised mopeds were only fun when the sun shone and not on rainy days but as training was being held in the managers house over in Mijas Golf I had

A NEW WIFE IN THE SUN

no choice but to clamber on board and hope that none of the other trainees thought I was incontinent when I walked into the room with a moist bottom.

Twenty minutes and several wrong turns later I finally located the property. Brushing the rain off my visor I stared up at the big detached house then down at my sodden attire. A knot formed in my stomach as I gingerly reached out to push the doorbell on the gate.

Hesitating, I let my hand stay mid air. Uncertainty gripped me and the bell remained untouched. Clutching my helmet, I bowed my head and turned back towards the bike. Whom was I kidding; this dog was way too old to learn new tri.....

The door behind me suddenly opened and a masculine voice cut through the air

"Hola! You must be Paula. Come in!"

PLOTS LANDING

"**A**nd just to summarise, the libro del edificio must be handed over before completion. Is everyone clear on that?"

Several heads nod in agreement and chat animatedly about the merits of real estate protocol. The middle aged French lady sat next to me on the sofa is rapidly taking notes on ipad but all I can feel in my hands is the glimmer of perspiration alongside the heavy weight of responsibility.

Gazing forlornly out the window I realise how easy Estate Agents must have it back in the UK. All they have to do is sit in a nice cosy office, sipping cappuccinos and pointing out the advantages of having a combi boiler and a South facing rear patio to mortgage eager customers

Here in Andalucía the process is slightly different. Not only do you have to source the property by pounding the streets, craning your neck for 'Vende' boards which appear to be written in Crayola, you then also have to make contact with the owner via phone or smoke signals in their native tongue then try and convince them that paying 5% of the asking price for an agent to market their home is the only viable option if they genuinely want to sell their home before the inevitable apocalypse occurs. Only after all this has been agreed and signed in blood, sweat and fears you begin to research all the relative information and debts associated with the property which invariably involves 13 siblings and an ancient Micmac burial ground nestling beneath the Bougainvilleas.

"I think that's enough information for one day. Let's head over to a site that's currently being built on and liaise with the developers over a glass of wine" yells our invigorated sales leader.

My ears suddenly prick up and I grab my handbag in anticipation of the hard earned liquid refreshment on offer. Several trainees from the group pile into a sign written Fiat Punto and we head off in the direction of Marbella. I look out the window and wonder if there will be any unadopted sandwiches to accompany the fluids we have been promised just as my stomach complains loudly about its lack of contents.

"Here we are!" yells our enthusiastic mentor and I look outside only to be greeted by a large span of wasteland with several people in suits standing proudly, pointing into the empty space whilst clutching glasses of chilled champagne, smiling with commission purchased teeth.

I heave my ample buttocks out of the confines of the car and stand uncertainly on the perimeter of the nothingness. A man with a mahogany tan comes forward and places a glass of something sparkling in my hand then starts to converse with the rest of the group in Spanish. I try and make myself less conspicuous by nodding occasionally whilst sipping the contents of my liquid lunch.

Looking around at the other candidates I suddenly realise that a) I have nothing in common with anyone here apart from the fact we are all breathing and b) I don't care about square footage or deeds or who owns the right to the footpath to the left of the gravel. I don't care about making pots of money or having a fancy car. I care about having a bit of fun in the sun and doing what I do best, which in all honesty, isn't much.

The developer finally stops talking and everyone shakes his hand and pats him on the back. For all I know he could have been discussing the dimensions of the 'new and improved' Prisoner Cell Block H. My stomach rumbles in anguish over its lack of solid contents and I make my excuses and head over to a group of people that may or may not be holding plates. On closer inspection they are surrounding a man who is slicing a giant ham with gusto so I stand in line, pointing greedily at the carcass and my mouth begins to water in anticipation as he piles the meat onto my plate. Grabbing several pieces of bread from a nearby table I head off alone to find a decent size piece of rubble to sit upon. Balancing the food on my knee, I cram the bread into my mouth and turn my face towards the sun.

"So, how are you finding training?" bellows a male voice from overhead.

Attempting to swallow, but without success I nod my head in what I hope looks like an enthusiastic motion and wave my arms around me to denote my agreement over the luxury apartments that are to be built upon this barren land. The man nods and smiles then heads back towards the eager crowd and I sit alone, wiping my greasy fingers on a napkin, knowing full well that this frock, on a rock, with her hock will absolutely, undoubtedly, undeniably not be returning tomorrow, or any other day to pursue a career in real estate.

All that's left to do now is inform my husband of this decision...

TELEHUBBIES

"**S**o, let me get this right…you spent the afternoon in a field, quaffing chilled white wine while intermittently stuffing your trap with iberico ham as the sun beat down on your botoxed brow, talking crap to a gaggle of creosote realtors and it was at that precise point you suddenly decided, in your imminent wisdom, that doing absolutely nothing in the middle of a nowhere wasn't the right career path for you? Paula, what DO you actually want to do work wise because we are running out of options here!!?"

Avoiding eye contact with my ever patient spouse I raise my shoulders in a non committal shrug and rotate the anemic looking chicken around the frying pan one more time. At the ripe old age of 51 I still have no idea what I want to be when I grow up but I do know that I never want to be thought of as normal or, in this case, an estate agent.

The doorbell suddenly bites through the uncomfortable silence and my husband shakes his head in my general direction then rushes over to invite a long awaited guest inside our home. Placing the spatula onto the kitchen worktop I wipe the mid August sweat of my forehead and plant a forced smile on my reticent lips.

A tanned giant of a man suddenly blocks the light cascading through the door and I notice that our visitor is clutching what looks like a satellite dish. His face looks vaguely familiar but before I have chance enquire my husband interjects.

"Paula, this is Dan the TV man. In a short while he's promised to reacquaint me with my old friend Jeremy Clarkson" and promptly whoops in delight at the prospect of finally having Freeview British TV installed in our home.

Dan, the aforementioned man, catches my eye and lazily smiles in an 'I have a large piece of equipment and I'm not afraid to use it' sort of way and I suddenly realize that the peace residing in our humble home would be no more. Conversation becoming nothing but a distant memory, early nights cast aside in favour of Keith Lemon's antics.

"Anyone fancy a cuppa?" I say to the two retreating backs, but silence greets my liquid invitation.

"Please yourselves", I mumble to no one in particular and flick a cobweb off my inherited Spanish chandelier. Brian farts and rolls over, staring at me with his strange almond eyes and dribbles on my BHS slippers. I sigh and watch the men folk pointing skywards on the terrace and sucking air between their teeth as they both point out inappropriate spots for the dish to take up residence.

Within minutes the huge white metal umbrella has been installed high upon the wall and our tanned entertainment messiah, nodding his head in approval promptly goes in search of the lounge. At a loss as what to do now, both of us trail after him like silent apostles and sit quietly on the sofa while he works his magic on our dust covered flat screen, forcing us out of the Spanish technology doldrums and back into the future.

The television that had sat for so many months in enforced solitude suddenly roars back into life and we are instantly greeted with the familiar face of Fiona Bruce waxing lyrical about one elderly gent's inherited Ming vase which turns out to be a fake and is actually worth the same price as a bag of Wotsits.

"Well that's your lot, I'll see myself out. If you want anything else give me a call, I've got fingers in many pies.... be it Chicken or Kidney".

At the mention of this Northern Delicacy Brian's ears suddenly perk up but my husband is sat transfixed by the television, lost in a world of heirlooms and disappointments.

 I make my way to the front door to bid farewell to our latest tradesman and once again I'm struck by how familiar his face appears to be.

"I can't place who you remind me of?" I say as he struggles down the stairs, his arms loaded with cable and tools.

With a cheeky grin he turns, grins and replies 'Tom Cruise?' and at that precise moment Dan the TV Man misses a step, stumbles and goes tumbling down the few remaining stairs, equipment showering down around him as he hits the marble floor with an unceremonious thump.

'Its fine, I'm fine' he yells upstairs and I stifle a smile as he stumbles out into the afternoon sunshine.

Suddenly it comes to me, who he reminds me off, I yell at his retreating figure " Garlic BREAD!"

PETERS AND ME

"**N**o dahhhling you have to chase Billy around the table THREE times, swing left, punch right and then have a cigarette. Make notes in your script if you can't remember" yells the director

"But... but you told me yesterday to do it the other way round?" I shout uncertainly into the dazzling spotlight but my reply is met with a deafening silence so I wander back into the wings and join the other cast members who are sat laughing at the confused look etched onto my weary face.

"Don't worry, that's what he does" whispers the elder of my on-stage sons "he changes his mind and then blames us. Don't waste time questioning it. He's been directing here for over 30 years and he isn't going to change"

Sighing with resignation I reach down for my script, erase all my previous notes and scrawl my new ones onto the rapidly disintegrating paper. Looking out onto the stage I see the young male lead circling the stage with his imaginary kestrel and wonder, not for the first time why I put myself through this unpaid torture.

From a very early age I required verification that I was indeed, different. I would perform comedy sketches to strangers on the tram after our weekly shop at 'Quick Save'. My mum would struggle up several flights of stairs as I gave my rendition of 'Paper Roses' to anyone that would listen and after a particularly torturous trip on the 11C bus to exchange some broken Hoover parts, she finally decided to give someone else's ears a bashing and entered me into a local talent show hosted by Uncle Peter Webster.

This legendary seaside show was the highlight of the Blackpool summer season. Hundreds of proud parents would watch the fruit of their loins destroy some harmonious melody or tap dance themselves off the stage. The winner being decided by the audience members so the more family you coerce with the promise of Dandelion and Burdock and Pork scratchings, the better your chances became.

Unfortunately, if you were entered in a heat with an Irish child you may as well just cut your losses and head home with your stick of consolation Rock. With so many Leprechauns attending the show they had to sit on each other's laps and fists would fly if 'Baby Connors' tuneless horn-Pipe rendition wasn't met with adoring applause from the surrounding parents.

The highly desired prizes lined the glistening stage, sat in untouchable supremacy. Dolls houses and giant teddy bears fought for dominance while eager contestants stood nervously wringing chubby sticky fingers, their dreams being held in a stranger's hand, awaiting their names to be called from the wings.

It was on a summers afternoon in 1972 that my 5 year old skinny and confident body marched itself onto the stage and sang 'Where's your mama gone' to a packed audience and amazingly, chirpy chirpy cheep cheeped my way to first prize which was a shock even to me as I was sure the blind 7 year old piano player would pip me to the post with his Liberace tribute act.

Deafening applause greeted my return to the winning stage and I briefly caught the shocked but proud look on my mother's face, no doubt imaging her future self having to trail to auditions in the wind and rain with her very own Lena Zavaroni incarnate doing vocal exercises on the last bus to Bispham.

Uncle Peter Webster held out his hand to take mine for our bows but I bypassed the smiling compare and headed straight towards the row of gleaming prizes. Without hesitation I clutched A giant purple doll to my chest which was almost the same height as me and yelled 'look mum I've won' into the audience. Laughter surrounded us and from that moment on I knew I was never going to be normal.

A rapid prod in the back brought me out of my 1970's reverie and I was dragged back into a world where strangers were no longer called uncle and dolls that yelled 'Mama' when tipped forward have been eagerly replaced with technology and flashing lights.

"Mum, can I have a few Euros; I'm not in this next scene and I'm FAMISHED and I remembered ALL my lines, unlike you", my son says with a cheeky smile

Reaching into my pocket I drag out whatever change I have and watch my boy, all gangly 12 years of him confidently run out of the door, not a care in this world, adamant that a future onstage is where his heart lies.

Mrs Casper - Kes
(Image by Graham Spencer Photography)

Stretching and reaching for my script I catch sight of myself in the mirror. My mother's eyes look back at me and I realize now, I'm in the same situation as she was all those years ago, a parent with a child who holds dreams of stardom in their hearts.

"Act 1 beginners to stage please, beginners to stage"

Brushing my wilting beehive back from my aging brow, I paint a frown onto my working class face and do what I do best, pretend to be somebody else.

DIVAN INTERVENTION

"**W**hat on earth is a blanket trip and who in their right mind needs blankets? It's almost 30 degrees out there and it's not even 8am!"

Blotting the sweat which is trickling at an unhealthy speed down into my cleavage, I explain once again to my confused husband what my latest form of employment actually is.

"It's not just blankets, its mattresses too and they are all made from the best Marino wool that ewe can buy. Anyway, I'm more than happy for you to find me my dream job, just as I found you YOURS in the theatre!" and I slam the door behind me and head for the stairs.

Unfortunately my dramatic exit is cut short when I tentatively have to reopen the door to retrieve my forgotten helmet and then slam it for a second time.

Mumbling to myself, I gingerly place my buttocks on the already blisteringly hot moped seat and head towards my latest form of employment.

I'd spotted the job advertised online a couple of weeks earlier and it sounded relatively easy. All you were required to do was stand in a hotel foyer and book people onto free locals excursions. The only catch being before you reached the chosen destination; a detour was made to watch a well presented sales pitch led by two charismatic women in a factory outlet in Malaga. All this was made more enticing by the fact there wasn't actually any hard sell on the beds and coffee and cake was provided along with a glass of sherry.

The promoters were so passionate about the products I was almost swayed to purchase a mattress and a pair of wool innersoles myself but then remembered I needed neither and in all honesty, had no money left for such frivolity. But several pensioners did purchase the products and the mood was good humored as we left the factory and headed towards Mijas village for the complimentary day out.

A car horn suddenly beeps loudly behind me and I realize that the traffic light has changed from Red to Green. Within minutes I am parked outside my local hotel and straighten my crumpled blouse before heading into the embrace of the air conditioned building.

"Blanket trips anyone? Free trip to a Ranch afterwards, tapas and drinks included...plus a free stallion if you can fit it in your hand luggage" I smile at the elderly guests making their way to breakfast. Some look at me as if I'm trying to sell them funeral plans but others happily sign up with the promise that the sales pitch in the factory isn't hard and the coach is air conditioned. Every signature on the sheet contributes towards my pay along with the knowledge that I will start Tour Guiding on the coach once a position becomes available.

The morning finally draws to a close and I pack up my clipboard along with my sales pitch and head home, stopping en route to pick up some fresh bread from the Panaderia.

Opening the apartment door I immediately hear the voice of

my son yelling into his Xbox alongside the dulcet tones of Jeremy Clarkson omitting from the lounge. Placing the still warm rolls on the counter I await confirmation of my return but I wait alone, technology taking precedent over human contact.

As I stand forlornly by the vibrating fridge I am struck by the realization that my son isn't suddenly going to start playing in the streets with the local Spanish children, he's almost a teenager and the online forums are now his virtual playground. My husband quite happily works in a local theatre; he isn't ever going to be the next Bill Gates. He enjoys lighting the luvvies and in his spare time watching middle aged men drive fast cars and talk crap and get paid millions to wax lyrical about Ford Mustangs.

Retracing my steps, I pick up my keys and retreat back to the front door. But blocking my path is the one family member that's always pleased to see me, Brian the ever hopeful. Shaking in anticipation he reaches up to me with his dirty paws and looks me in the eye, happy in the knowledge that he has a warm bed to sleep in, food in his bowl every night and most importantly, people that love him.

"Maybe we should all be more like you Brian, grateful for what we have' I whisper to my furry companion and he replies by gratefully licking my nose. Picking up his lead we head outside into the fresh air and away from the internal noise. Moving to Spain was my dream and the reality of the situation isn't easy. Work is vastly underpaid, families still argue, the language is a barrier but the one thing that there is here in abundance is sunshine and cheap wine, and that brightens even the darkest of moods.

"Fancy a sausage sandwich?" I enquire to my four legged friend and he replies with a wag of his tail. Smiling to myself I cross the road and head into the shade, just another expat strolling the avenue whilst trying her best to find a new life in the sun.

BANGER MANAGEMENT

(6 months later)

"**N**o seriously, does my arse really look like a giant blue beach ball in this TUI uniform?"

My husband, always grateful that the subject matter isn't about doing any more unnecessary DIY in the apartment turns towards me and looks me carefully up and down

"It's definitely more flattering than the yellow one you wore last year on that bed promotion thing you did. Anyway, stop preening or you'll be late on your first day. Have you charged the tablet up and downloaded all those Apps?"

I nod nervously. Me and technology aren't the closest of allies. I can work out Face Book, E mails and how to buy crap on Amazon but apart from that I'm useless. My palms start to sweat with the thought of a thousand unhappy tourists staring at me while I jab helplessly at a computer screen that insists on saying 'transaction not recognised!'

Looking into the mirror I smooth down the man made fibers and hoist the Rep bag over my shoulder. Amongst all the truly talented bilingual candidates, 51 year old me was offered the position of part time representative for TUI in one of the biggest hotels in Fuengirola and I was not going to let my larger than average posterior put me off my new career.

"Right, I'm off then, see you after you finish work at the Theatre" and I happily head downstairs to my trusty Vespa.

Within ten minutes I'm standing uncertainly outside the entrance of the hotel. I had worked the same place last season, but that was promoting free blanket trips to elderly people but this season I was the face of TUI. The buck stops with me. Painting a smile on my heavily made up face I march through the front door and spot my Team leader lounging on the sofa, writing out welcome packs.

Clearing my throat I hold out my hand and become the person I know the company wants me to be.

"Hello, I'm Paula; I'm your part time team mem...."

"Whoa whoa whoa...Part time? Part time? I need a full time rep here, this just isn't on!" and with my hand left hanging in mid air the unsmiling portly Tui rep grabs his works phone and marches past me through the front door and out of sight into the street.

This wasn't exactly the reaction I had been hoping for so I stand uncertainly by the desk, fingering the various flyers and looking at the airport departure board for divine inspiration.

"Oh hello, can you help me?" an elderly voice cuts through my reverie

Pasting a smile upon my lips I turn around to see a lady of about 90 years old sporting a tiny fluorescent bikini and wearing the brightest pink lipstick (albeit mainly on her teeth) that I have ever seen.

"I appear to have lost my husband. I sent him down to get me a sausage over half an hour ago and he's not returned to the room. They ran out of sausages yesterday, I had to have bacon, I don't like bacon, to be honest, I don't really like sausages but I don't like to queue for an omelet"

Placing a look of concern on my face I nod in sympathy but before I have chance to solve this modern day dilemma I see my colleague march back in through the front door, anger etched into his olive skin.

"Er..... This lady appears to have lost her husband on the way to the buffet breakfast; he went for a sausage and hasn't been seen since." I smile beseechingly for help from my mentor; I'm not yet au-fait with the protocol of missing OAP's, or the lack of re-formed Pork if I'm honest.

"Have you looked in the lift Mrs. P? He was in there yesterday morning wasn't he? Talking to the chambermaid on the 14th-floor about the benefits of Aloe Vera?'"

The guest looked confused and then realization dawned like the early morning sun through heavily advancing hazy clouds.

"Oh so he was, I'll go and have a look for him up there, I do hope my sausage hasn't gone cold though...." and off she wanders, mumbling to herself about pork products and wayward husbands.

I turn to my colleague who has resumed his position on the sofa and take a deep breath

"Look, I don't know what you were expecting but I can promise you this, I'll work hard and the guests will love me. Surely it's better to have a really good part timer than an utterly rubbish full time one?"

He looks at me through narrowed eyes then takes a deep breath of resignation.

"Those welcome packs won't fill themselves"

Smiling to myself I lift the mountain of leaflets from the table, salute with a cheeky grin and get to work.

TUI STORY

"**G**ood morning, welcome to the Hotel Yarimar, I'm your TUI team leader and my job here is to make sure you all have a fantastic holiday here in Fuengirola"

So the welcome speech begins once again. I'm sat watching from the sidelines, smiling like a Madame Tussaud's waxwork and trying not to spill the complimentary Orange Juice down my blouse. There are six of us clad in Blue, awaiting our introduction alongside the Blanket Trip representative, sporting a canary yellow ensemble, whom I fear may nod off before our team leader even reaches the merits as to why you need to book your trips with us as opposed to the half price bucket shop down the road.

I look around the room. The average age of the clientele is around 93 and there's no guarantee all of them will make it to the end of the 50 minute speech. The air conditioning unit wheezes into life and jolts awake several elderly patrons, reminding them they are on holiday and need to stay conscious for at least some of their pensioner's vacation.

I catch the eye of one of the entertainments team and we wink at each other in unison. These youngsters are the glue that holds the hotel together, performing West End worthy shows in the evening after a day of interacting with the guests in various activities around the pool. They know the score; all of them have been hired following extensive auditions in the UK to ensure everyone has a great time onsite. Scores for the hotel must remain high because if they chose to do another season with Tui, their next curtain call could be in Florida as opposed to Fuengirola. Point's makes prizes; the constant carrot dangled in front the TUI employee's nose.

I'm sure when they applied for the roles; wide eyed and fresh out of drama school they didn't envisage a day of shuffleboard and French boules adorning their crispy white untarnished CV but this is the reality of most actors worlds and like all professionals, they rise to the occasion with a smile and a caffeine laden drink.

I look up towards the ceiling and wipe sweat off my menopausal brow. The meeting is well into its stride. Pickpockets and prickly heat have been touched upon, train timetables are being hastily noted down on welcome packs and we are rapidly heading towards the bread and butter of the speech, excursions.

I think back to the past month and try and remember which

inland adventures I have attended, each one morphing into the next. Museums, mosques, mountains, information overload.

Sitting on a coach at 8am each morning, watching the younger reps vomit into their rucksacks after an alcohol fuelled outing the night before. Patting their inexperienced backs and trying to keep them away from the incredibly young area manager who joined us each day on the tours. Fighting the desire to yell 'I've got cheese in my fridge older than you' whenever he pointed out an obvious fact regarding how we were expected to behave in front of the paying guests also on the tour.

"And now Paula is going to come up and tell you about Romantic Ronda! Gentleman, you can go to sleep now".

My name breaks through the deluge of memories and drags me back into reality. I stand up and brush invisible crumbs of my skirt and head over to the rostrum and smile encouragingly towards my ever deflating audience. All these people who sit before me have come for a nice holiday and not to listen to middle aged reps wax lyrical on how they should spend their money. With this in mind I take a deep breath and perform a short comedy monologue on Riotous Ronda and then return to my seat, applause rings around the room as the team leader brings the meeting to a close.

Dragging my Tablet out of the bag I fire it up and stand at the table nearest to exit awaiting the arrival of any guests that fancy spending their hard earned cash on a trip to Morocco or Marbella.

An elderly lady pushes her way through the ever decreasing crowd and waves a shaky finger in my direction

"Jane Macdonald, that's who you remind me off, I bloody love her on that cruise programme"

Smiling I lean down and whisper conspiratorially "It's a shame I haven't got her money. Now, can I interest you in a nice day trip to see the apes in Gibralter?"

A TAIL OF TWO BICCIES BY BRIAN CROFT

S he's putting on that sky coloured outfit again, the one that smells of sausages and old people. It must be her favourite thing ever as she wears it most days now, although it does get taken off each night and hurled into that big white noisy thing which spins crazily around the kitchen until it exhausts itself. She opens it's mouth and the dress comes out smelling of flowers! I like flowers. I like to wee on flowers but I don't wee on her dress because I know when she comes back from that place she calls her 'work' the outfit will smell like it did before she put it in the hungry thing; like pensioners, pancakes and Paula.

I'm watching her from my chair. She looks smiley and is humming as she puts some bright red stuff on her mouth and brushes her hair. I love my mum. She lets me have bits of food when she is cooking and takes me for a swim in the sea when everyone else is still asleep. When we come back dad stands with his hands on his hips and says 'Has he been on that beach again? You know you'll get fined if they catch him on there' but mum just shrugs and helps herself to a biscuit from a big jar. She sometimes talks to the biscuits saying they are naughty just before she eats them. I like naughty biscuits.

I stretch and put my legs in the air. I have my own armchair. It's very comfortable. I sometimes try and sit on other peoples big chairs but I'm not allowed because apparently I shed which confuses me as I'm a Brian, not a shed. No one sits on my chair but me and occasionally silly strangers who walk in and plonk themselves down on it. When they get up they look annoyed as there's a lot of me on them apparently. I don't mind, they can share me and my shed.

My mum pats me on the head and then goes out the door and gets on that shiny blue thing with 2 wheels that I think is called 'Be careful!' Dad shouts that whenever mum is on it but she just waves and overtakes cars. Dad shakes his head. Dad does that a lot when mum is on 'Be careful'. My brother asked if he could have a 'be careful' when he's older and mum said something about it being over her dead body. My brother then slammed the door and my mum ate another biscuit.

Dad farts in the bedroom. I get down off my comfy chair and wander in to see him. He pats me on the head and says 'Do you want to come with me to work today?' and I wag my bottom. We both have breakfast. Dad never has any of mine but I sometimes get some of his as he drops crumbs when talking to mum on his little black box. She makes dad laugh. He calls her a pain in the arse but is smiling when he says this.

"Go and get your lead then" dad says putting the talky machine down but I'm already at the front door, waiting and wagging. I like the park, it has a lot of smells and I like to potter about but Dad walks around behind me sighing and telling me to hurry up, holding a sandwich bag as we've run out of MY bags apparently. Once I've recycled my breakfast on the grass we head towards the big noisy building with lots of chairs and a stage where everyone's name is 'Darling'. I quite like it here. Lots of people pat me on the head when I walk through and sometimes I find a misplaced crisp on the floor. My dad works here in the night making everyone look shiny. Mum says he pushes buttons for a living but dad just gives her 'the look' and says if she wants to look shiny next time she's on stage then she better stop pushing his buttons. Mum just laughs, she likes pushing his buttons herself sometimes. I like chocolate buttons but I'm not allowed them.

Me and my man pet go outside and sit with some smiley people with skin resembling my chew bone. They pat dad on the back and ask him to make sure that they look FABULOUS on stage. I tilt my head; I didn't know dad was a magician too. Good job my mum wasn't here, she would snort into her drink and dad would have to kick her under the table.

I can feel my eyes growing heavy, the air is getting really warm now and I close my eyes and lie down under the table. When I was very small mum got very sad as I have something called Hip Dysplasia. She says we moved to Spain for me as it would make me feel better as being cold made my legs hurt a lot.

As I drift off to sleep, surrounded by the laughter of strangers I sigh and remember how very lucky I am to be a New Bri in the Sun.

A BARD DAYS NIGHT

"**S**o in total that will be 418 Euros for the three excursions for three people, are you paying cash or card?"

I never thought as myself as much of a sales person before starting our Andalucían adventure but it appears I'm really rather good at making money for TUI. Swiping the MasterCard through the wireless machine with a flourish, the transaction is instantly confirmed and I hand the coach tickets over to the sun kissed tourists and watch as the more elderly of the two adventurers carefully places the receipts underneath her bikini top for 'safe keeping'.

Stretching, I look up at the hotel reception clock and realize I should have finished work over half an hour ago. Reaching over to my flipchart, I carefully write what daylight hours I will be working the following day and make my way out the front door, bidding farewell to the doe eyed Spanish cleaners as I leave.

'Be Careful' is sat waiting patiently in the MOTO bay alongside several other battered steeds and I hastily fire her ancient engine up. Gingerly I place my continuously ample buttocks upon the scorching black leather seat and roar off down the seafront, trying to avoid the impromptu stag party which has taken up residence in the middle of the carriageway alongside their inflatable sheep and half consumed bottles of Jagermeister.

The beach is awash with sun seekers, greedily soaking up the heat and applying factor 50 to already pre baked skin. Children and pensioners sit side by side on pedalo's, trying to avoid teenagers on Jet Ski's who appear intent on never reaching their 21st birthdays.

Within minutes I'm parked outside my home and I happily make my way up the communal spiral stairs. The thermometer on the balcony has reached its peak and I let myself in the sweltering flat and drop my ruck sack on the floor while calling out a greeting to whichever inhabitants are still encased indoors.

My son, now age 13, has morphed from an outgoing young lad into a gangly monosyllabic teen who appears to have his phone surgically attached to his hand. Stumbling from the bedroom into the lounge he falls onto the sofa and without any acknowledgement of my previous absence, asks what's for lunch.

Sighing with parental resignation, I make my way into the circa 1973 kitchen and throw a few ingredients into the last two remaining slices of bread and add a couple of carrot sticks in way of compensation for my lack of culinary imagination. Grunting in my general direction, the 'Kevin' (minus Perry) incarnate staggers back into his bedroom clutching the food and slams the door without a backward glance, no doubt to resume destroying all of the undead on his Xbox1.

Slipping out of my 100% polyester ensemble I lazily head into the shower and let the cool water cascade down my rubenesque torso. Lathering my hair up into vosene frenzy I vow to start on my low carb diet once the weekend is over and after I've polished off the 2 scotch eggs hidden carefully at the back of the fridge.

Rubbing the soap along my unshaved Velcro legs I half heartedly hunt around for a razor then remember I used it to defluff the wayward bobbles on the sofa blanket the previous week. Closing my eyes under the spray I allow my mind to wander back over the past 16 months of our life in Spain and all the hurdles we've encountered and overcome, none of which was ever mentioned by the shiny eyed presenters on all of the relocation programmes back in the UK.

With resignation I turn the cold tap off and step out back into the humidity, patting myself dry and trying to avoid my middle aged naked reflection en route. Grabbing a sarong from behind the bathroom door I stroll into the lounge and immediately see my husband emptying his work bag on the table, shoulders hunched and lips devoid of whistle.

"You ok?" I ask without real concern, mind already subconsciously devouring the eggs of Scotchness.

"They've let me go"

"Whose let you go where?" I reply, confused, all thoughts of savoury products forgotten.

'The Theatre, they've let me go' he finally looks up, green eyes searching mine for an answer to his own question. "I've been made redundant".

NEPOTISM

"**S**o, let me get this right. You sauntered into work without a care in the world and 10 minutes later you were back pounding the pavements after being informed by Mary, Mongo and Midge from the board that you were suddenly surplus to requirement and that technology is now keeping your desk warm?"

The deflated form in front of me nodded and tried to rub the reality of the situation out of his confused eyes

"They can't do that, can they? I mean you have a contract, doesn't that count for anything?" desperation edged un-announced into my voice

"Well apparently they can and they have. I'm being made re-dundant, not sacked. They won't be allowed to employ anyone in my position though. Last in, first out. A computerised sys-tem is now sitting in my chair and drinking my espresso" he sighed with resignation.

Disbelief sat facing uncertainty, both of us not daring to voice our true concerns. We had bought a flat because of this job, put our son into a private school and made a life for ourselves, made friends; some true, and now it appeared, some false.

"Well I don't believe it. They can't just let you go without prior warning, there must be another reason. Is it because I wouldn't move my play to accommodate 'she who must be obeyed?'"

My mind wandered back to a couple of weeks earlier. I had been due to direct 'One Flew Over the Cuckoo's Nest' at the theatre but my 2020 November slot was being called into question. I'd heard through the Luvvie grapevine that someone higher up the theatrical food chain wanted to rearrange when their play was on so they could appear in their partner's production. Suddenly I was being 'requested' to accommodate. I enquired as to why a newcomer was being given such short shrift when surely new directing talent should be encouraged but I already knew the answer, nepotism.

Silence echoed around the increasingly claustrophobic lounge. My Tui uniform clung to me like a second skin. Looking down at my name badge I let out an audible sigh and tried to remain positive. At least I had my part time job to keep us afloat, sea-sonal as it was. I'd just have to make sure that my sales targets remained high so I would be brought back to work next sum-mer. I loved working in the hotel I had been allocated for the season. We had a wonderful and energetic entertainments team that the guests adored and even my reticent team leader had accepted that I was a good addition to the ensemble.

"So, what are you going to do now?" I enquired to my weary spouse "Do you have to go back in to the theatre to complete any unfinished jobs or is that it, Hasta Luego lighting guy?"

"I'm afraid that's it. They don't need me anymore, I'm officially unemployed. Anyway, it's been a hell of a morning, I'm going to take a shower then have a lie down, I've got a banging headache" and off he trudged, a shadow of his former optimistic self, confidence annihilated by a group of volunteers playing god.

Injustice raged through my vodka enhanced veins and I slumped down in front of my trusty laptop, exhausted by the change of events in our already uncertain expat lives. Only this time it wasn't the local authorities making our new life in the sun hard, it was the decisions of people we thought we knew and more importantly, trusted. The other Brits abroad.

Looking at the myriad of untapped letters hovering beneath my fingertips I paused for a moment, tilting my head to make sure that the noisy shower was indeed running. Thoughts cascaded around my brain like the water droplets no doubt drumming over my confused husbands shoulders. Moving to Spain didn't automatically entitle us all to a Happily Ever After...or did it?

Reaching for the keys without forethought, my impatient fingers took flight, replacing reality with fantasy while allowing creativity to combat negativity

'Once Upon A Time......'

Once Upon a Time A middle aged Prince and his menopausal wife moved to Fuengirola, In search of cheap wine and happy ever afters.

The prince was offered a position of lighting Technician in ye old theatre by an elderly enchantress and he went to work every day and night without complaint. The Prince was very happy, he loved lighting the luvvies. He was firmly cast under the thespian spell.

The stage was filled every month by different plays and musicals, wizened old queens performed in Panto and Fat ogres strutted across the boards, the audience clapped, the performers indulged.

One day, the Princes wife, a budding thespian herself was sat amongst the back patting fairy tale characters and interrupted the frivolity by declaring 'Can I possibly direct a play? I've done a few before'

The room became suddenly silent; no one had ever dared to ask this question before.

"Someone summon the board" bellowed one of the Queens henchmen while taking cover underneath a well used bar stool.

Loud steps could be heard overhead in the inner sanctum. Within moments the wife was surrounded by seven mismatched dwarves (although artistic license had been used as some of them were actually quite tall, but that's showbiz)

"Whose that trip tapping across my Bridge!!' yelled the most rotund of the ensemble

"Erm....I just wanted to know if I could direct a play, I'm really rather good even if I do say so myself, I could make the theatre some money" smiled the nervous wife.

The dwarves looked confused. Who was this interloper daring to try and invade their closed shop? The fattest of the dwarves stepped forward and growled into the face of the stunned wife

"This is the salon NON varieties; we don't have new people in our productions. We all want to be in everything ourselves and direct each other, that's the way it's always been, well, since we overthrew the last board because they wanted to direct themselves too!"

"OFF WITH HIS HEAD!!" yelled the wicked Queen and with a wave of her wand, the lighting technician was no more.

"Why are you obliterating my husband when it's me who asked the question" yelled the distraught wife

107

"Because we CAN!!!!" shouted the dwarves in unison!!!

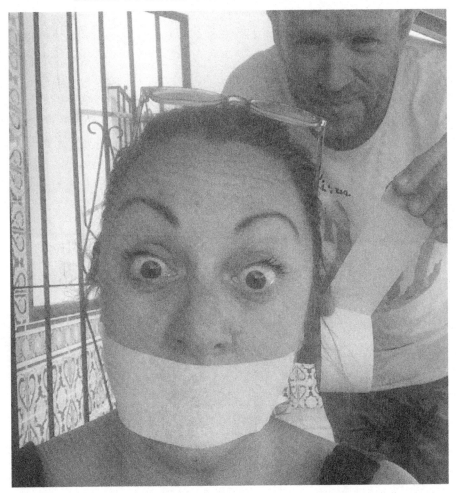

And the moral of this story? There is no happy ever after, just narcissists in Sunnyland.

MANGER THINGS

'Are you going to actually consume that final chipolata or are you just setting it up on a blind date with your last remaining sprout?'

My son nods, crams the remnants of his lunch into his mouth and then continues to sway to an unheard rhythm, Christmas Air-Pods stuck firmly in his ears, tapping his legs in time to whatever society dictates is music these days. I look over at my husband to share a conspiratorial smile but his head is also down, tapping at his phone screen whilst shaking his graying head in a Victor Meldrew fashion. An audible sigh escapes my lips and I reach across the dinner table to clear the festive plates away from the unresponsive pair. Another wishbone pulled, another dream unanswered, another day in the sun.

Brian 'the ever hopeful' is sat by the kitchen door, longingly staring up at the carcass of the ransacked turkey, tail wagging in anticipation of his own festive meal. I place the remnants of our plates into his bowl and he greedily devours the contents with canine glee.

My husband's voice breaks through the silence

"I've got a job on for tomorrow, a bloke in La Cala needs me to fix his Jacuzzi; he's got friends over for New Year and they are refusing to get in until it's got steam coming off it"

Once a lighting technician in the theatre, he had no choice but to return to being a jobbing electrician/handyman after redundancy stabbed him in the back. The manual labour he thought he had left behind was now part of his every waking day and each morning I listened to his bones creak like an old rocking chair left to the depredation of passing time.

My own adored job working for Tui as a resort rep was nothing but a distant seasonal memory. The powers that be decided to reward me for reaching (and exceeding) my monthly targets by removing me from the hotel I knew and loved and shoving me into an establishment that would give Stephen Kings 'Outlook Hotel' a run for its money. All that was required to complete this seafront vision was a frustrated writer with an axe and a pair of twins to haunt the corridors. The clientele, no longer tanned and affluent, had been replaced with elderly patrons insistent on having an ambulance on speed dial just in case the porridge wasn't heated to the required nuclear temperature. I spent most of my mornings hiding under the stairs, avoiding wheelchairs and inebriated pensioners with burnt tongues.

"What's for dessert mum? I'm still famished! Dad's eaten all the mince pies AGAIN and I'm not allowed any more After Eights"

I turn to look at my son and have to crane my neck upwards to speak him. Almost 6 foot now, all limbs and legs and attitude encased in teenage angst.

"I'll make you a fruit salad; you've had enough sweets today. Anyway, I thought you were meeting up with your friends at the skate park today? Go and see if they've messaged while I make dessert"

Turning to my husband I grab his glass of half finished wine from the table and motion for him to join me on the balcony. Outside in the street one of the local residents that we have fondly nick-named 'Crazy Jesus' is waving his arms about outside the Pan-aderia, shouting at invisible apostles whilst consuming a pastry encased in what looks like melted chocolate, pausing only to swallow a mouthful before his tirade of expletives continues.

I turn to look at my husband. He doesn't laugh a lot nowadays and I wonder, not for the first time if he is suffering from de-pression. Losing his job hit him hard, he loved lighting the luv-vies and watching each show evolve onstage. Now he was back to hauling tools around on his back and fixing other peoples botched electrics. He had stepped back in time with no tardis at hand to return to the future.

Taking a deep breath I voiced what had been on my mind for a while, the only solution to our ailing financial situation, a chance to begin again.

"I think we should sell the flat and buy a business and work for ourselves here on the coast…. and stop answering to fools"

I await his reply, it's a risk, a big risk, but isn't that why we moved out here in the first place?

Wary green eyes meet optimistic brown and a long forgotten dream suddenly resurfaces from behind a cloud of disappoint-ment. A smile reaches his lips, the first genuine one I've seen in a long time.

"Fuck it, let's do it, what's the worst that could possibly hap-pen?" and just like that, the Covid 19 spell was cast

A NEW STRIFE IN THE SUN - CORONAVIRUS: A BRIEF INTERLUDE

LOCKDOWN... DAY 1!

"It's my turn to walk Brian, you walked him last time! Where's his pet passport, have you hidden it?" My husband stares accusingly at me while I fiddle with my Lidl bag.

"It's where you left it, on top of the packing boxes, open your eyes!", I yell back through the bubble wrap.

It's March 15th and we have been ordered to stay indoors, which is a tad inconvenient seeing as though we are due to complete on our flat in 2 weeks time. We have already paid a deposit on rented accommodation and have committed to purchasing an ongoing business.

 All of this on the proviso that we complete on our flat on April the first. But there's one more fly in this ludicrous ointment, our buyers live in Denmark and unless they plan to swim over (which is forbidden as all the beaches in Spain have been shut) I have no idea how any of the above is going to be achievable.

Oh, and my son is due to start a new fee paying international school, did I mention that?

"Mum, can I go on my Play Station seeing as there's no school? It's a war game so it's kind of like studying History…"

I stare longingly at the bottle of Vodka nestled happily between the loaves of Bimbo bread. We have decided to give up alcohol until this whole pandemic is over but already I can feel my will-power slipping away, not unlike my good health if I decide to persue licking external door handles.

"Do we need anything from the supermarket while I'm walking the dog?" my spouse cheerily enquires.

"No! That's another day out, we can't combine the two! If you're walking the dog then I get to go to Iceland to buy Vimto and chat to the lady who calls everyone Sweetie", I reply… less cheerfully.

My husband frowns "are you allowed to go to Iceland? That's over the bridge, we have El Jamon closer, won't you get frog marched home by the lurgy police?"

I stare at the man I married. Does he not know me at all? How is a middle aged woman supposed to stay in enforced solitary confinement without a supply of Scotch eggs and a pack of frozen crumpets? If he thinks a man in uniform is going to come between me and my pack of overpriced Ginsters then he's sadly mistaken.

Grabbing my moped keys I make a bid for freedom out the front door. I have my passport, I have my Nie, I have my scarf wrapped round my face and my latex gloves on. I have my hastily sanitized 50 euro note.

"Have I forgotten anything?" I wheeze through my wool enclave as I turn at the door?

"Yes you have Paula, it's Sunday, and the supermarkets are shut!"

LOCKDOWN DAY 2

I'm having a lovely time with Hugh Jackman, sipping cocktails in his Jacuzzi while he tenderly massages my...

"Can't you hear the buzzer? I'm in the loo! It's the Amazon delivery... Hurry up or he'll go!"

I'm ripped out of my slumber by my husband yelling at me from the throne in the bathroom and I stagger out of bed and into the lounge whilst grasping my Dunelm dressing gown to my kebab friendly torso. I fling open the front door and I'm greeted by Darth Vader's older sibling who promptly thrusts out a brown box for me to take. I barely have time to ask if the force is with him before he disappears back down the communal stairs in a puff off sanitized dust.

Gently I place the familiar brown package on the table and go and unlock the balcony door. It's raining outside and the streets are eerily quiet. In the distance I can hear the hairy inhabitants of Biopark shouting for their breakfast and I look out onto the pavements for signs of life. The Panaderia across the road from us is open and a couple of people are stood outside it, keeping a respectful meter distance apart while they wait in line for fresh bread.

My husband, fresh from his ablutions, saunters into the lounge and stares at the box on the table and then at me.

"Have you washed your hands?"

I look at him enquiringly. I've not been anywhere to need to wash my hands. Then it dawns on me. The parcel, it could be holding a virus party all over its exterior, an invisible germ rave.

Shaking my head I head over to the sink and destroy yet another layer of my skin with washing up liquid and boiling hot water then pat them dry on my dressing gown.

"I'm going to walk Brian over to the office after breakfast, give the props another coat of paint, are you coming? You'll have to walk behind me if you do, take a shopping bag so it looks like your off to get supplies" he enquires.

"Why don't you just get me a red cape too and I can pretend I'm an extra in The Handmaid's Tale? I'll yell 'Unclean Unclean' just to make the walk more interesting if you like?"

My husband, used to my frustrated outbursts, just ignores my sarcastic comments and makes himself another coffee.

"What's in the box anyway" I mumble, in way of an apology.

"It's that projector we ordered for the office entrance hall. I'm going set it up tonight in the lounge and we use it like a cinema screen until the business opens....."

Ah yes, the 'New' business. Have I told you about what that is? No? I'll get round to that...

LOCKDOWN DAY 3 & 4

D^{AY 3}

"Get off that bloody Play Station and brush the dog, there's tumbleweeds of hair everywhere"
"Why?"

"Because I say so!"

"Why can't Dad do it?"

"Dad is busy!"

"No he's not. He's watching Star Trek and eating custard creams"

"Are you eating the last of the Biscuits?"

"No....."

"We need to start packing soon Marcus, just in case we complete on April fool's day, can you get the stuff off the top of the wardrobe?"

"I will, after Spock saves the Enterprise from the Tribble"

"*sigh* ...I'm cooking lunch in a minute, can you both set the table? Hello, hello? Oh fu*k it, you can get your own bloody food, I'm going back to bed!"

DAY 4

"That cloud looks like a sausage dog; look it's got one leg shorter than the other"

I am sat on the balcony with my husband. All attempts at personal grooming have vacated the building and I'm slowly starting to resemble Waynetta's uglier sibling. The bathroom, in desperate need of a damp sponge and a vat of bleach, waits patiently while Facebook and WhatsApp take precedence over household chores. Nobody is coming to visit us any more so why bother?

"I think I'll walk Brian over to the office, make sure everything is ok, no leaks or power cuts" my husband mumbles to no one in particular.

The "Office" is the term we use for our new business and is on the street behind us. We daren't say the name of it just in case armageddon actually occurs and we never get to open. Weeks have been spent renovating the existing template but now it's just sat there, waiting to be explored, lonely in its enforced isolation. When will it be full of curious customers? Only this virus knows the answer. We no longer get to dictate our lives, an invisible force is playing hide and seek with our waking days and time is the only master.

I look up the sky, the sausage dog has gone. It's just a blanket of grey enveloping the landscape.

"Grab a bottle of Vodka on your way back," I say to the departing figure, "I think we are going to need it."

DAY 21 (504 HOURS... 30,240 MINUTES... 1,814,400 SECONDS).

I can't physically see my feet anymore. Where have they gone? Has someone kidnapped them along with my sense of humour? I'm sure they were there 3 weeks ago. I try and suck the mottled beach ball in that has taken up residence just above my hips but it just reveals a couple of chipped orange toenails.

Squinting into the mirror I don't recognize the puffed up face staring back at me. I look like the Pillsbury dough boys granny. My hair hasn't moved position from the scrunchie I wrapped it up in 3 days ago. I tilt my head and it remains static, a monument to apathy.

My dressing gown has become this seasons essential item; worn throughout the day, only to be removed when Brian needs to perform his ablutions and only then is it peeled off my reluctant torso to be replaced with my 'I love disco' onesie which is now my dog walking 'no more than 50 yards or you'll get fined' outfit of choice.

A prolonged fart omits from the kitchen area. A tall middle aged figure is stood filling up the kettle staring blankly at the tiles. He's rarely seen before noon; an apprentice Nescafé vampire in 80's underwear. The only reason he rises at all is to fulfill his yearning for caffeine which is usually enough of an energy boost to propel him into another room. Once the relocation of choice has been decided upon, seldom does he rise again until the battery on his phone dies or he runs out of digestives.

My son, infrequently seen out of his bedroom at the best of times, can be heard yelling into his headset throughout the day until the time comes when he is dragged out to the terrace to reluctantly run his enforced 100 laps and then returns to his den of inactivity to resume the position, promising to shower at some later date, probably sometime in June if we still have enough gas in the canister.

My long days are filled with a series of stimulating observations and conversations

"That women at number 23 has been out twice today, she didn't even have a shopping bag with her the second time"

"Do you want cheese AND ham in your sandwich? I'm not risking Iceland again, I'll probably get taken out on the bridge by a sniper if he sees me foraging for cheddar again"

"Can you flip me over if I haven't moved in the next 12 hours, the bedsores are starting to antagonize my cellulite"

"Shut the F*ck up, I want a divorce... not that we'll have any money left at the end of this"

And so it goes on... our enforced isolation. The world is holding its terrified breath awaiting a time when we are allowed to walk freely along our chosen foreign shores and dip our toes back into normality again.

But today is not that day and nor is tomorrow, or next week for that matter.

I sigh and rearrange my face into one that isn't terrified for my child's future.

'Right, who fancies a game of Trivial Pursuit? Winner gets to take the bins out!!'

DAY... WHO THE F#CK KNOWS?

Pi$$ed-off Packing Mama

I'm staring vacantly at the contents of the wardrobe. Who owns all these clothes? They can't be mine, I can't fit my right thigh through most of them.

My size 10 wedding dress, clad in polythene, stands upright commanding centre stage and seemingly awaiting a marital ovation. I sigh in resignation and clip a feathered fascinator to my greasy locks and start to remove several forlorn dresses from the plastic hangers and dump them into an open bin bag.

"Don't go throwing everything away because you can't be arsed packing," yells my husband from the lounge.

A vivid image of a bubble wrapped torso being hurled from the balcony suddenly springs to mind but I shake the thought away. We haven't got enough of the popping packaging to even finish the glassware never mind a 6ft struggling spouse.
I sigh again. I hate moving. No that's a lie, I love moving I just

hate packing.

My son walks in and stares blankly at the bin bags, then honours me with speech.

"Next time we move can we pay someone to pack for us? This looks like the leftovers from a crappy car-boot sale, what's to eat?" I stare at my gangly offspring; aged 14 and still completely unaware that we are due to move apartments in just 5 days.

The phone suddenly rings. It's the estate agent.

"Hi Carmen, any news?"

"Hello Paola, can you send me a video of your flat when it's empty, including the locks"

"Why do you need a video of the locks? We're not going to come back and start squatting!!!" I roll my eyes and wait for a reply. When none is forthcoming I ask the same question I've asked a hundred times this week.

"So, have you been able to contact the police and ask them if we are actually ALLOWED to move this weekend because I'm going to be a bit pissed off if I'm thrown in jail en route to the notary." Silence echoes down the phone. Our conversation is seemingly complete.

"Marcus! They've hung up on me again," I yell into the lounge and my voice echoes around the empty room.

Our Spanish estate agent is apparently more than happy to take the 6% commission on the sale of our property but appears unwilling to take any responsibility regarding our transition from A-B, albeit being less than a mile between destinations.

The lack of control sits uneasily astride my nomadic feet. Visions of S.W.A.T teams descending on us as we load Tupperware into the removal van suddenly fills my overactive and under stimulated brain. Lockdown has disabled us all from the most simple of tasks and I feel tears prick at the back of my eyes. Self pity isn't a welcome companion when airports are being used as morgues around the globe and I remind myself of this as I hurl our future into an assortment of cardboard boxes.

A comforting hand touches my shoulder, disrupting the unwelcome thoughts cascading around my frazzled brain.

"'The Noodle bar downstairs has just opened, I heard the shutter go up. You fancy something hot and spicy? I'm sure they will deliver, even if we do only live 4 metres away."

I look at him. The elephant is sitting quite clearly in the room and for once it's not me. Clearing my throat I open up the can of worms we've been keeping locked away.

"Marcus, I think we need to talk about the business we've just bought"

KNOW ESCAPE

"**S**o what happens now, do we just loose the 4K deposit, or do we take the gamble on Covid19 being a temporary blip and just steam ahead regardless?"

My husband is looking into my eyes for answers but for once in my life, I'm all out of opinion.

Our renewed employment optimism began when I chanced upon a business venture for sale earlier on this year; something we could easily run between ourselves that didn't involve a deep fat fryer or the need to be polite to inebriated Brits; something that would fulfill our theatrical requirements and bring home the Iceland (overpriced) bacon.

But I'm jumping ahead...

It was a chilly winter's morning and I'd been happily strolling over to El Jamon with my trusty old-lady trolley. I decided to take a detour along a tree-lined side street when I glanced up to see an unremarkable grey wall with some strange hieroglyphics stenciled upon it. Upon further inspection it appeared to be some kind of shop and I gingerly peered in through the frosted glass.

Being both curious, and more than a tad nosy, I tapped on the shuttered door and was met by a non-Spanish blonde lady who welcomed me in.

'What is this place?' I asked, looking around at the internal doors which all had timer's placed above them. 'Is it a speed brothel??'

The lady smiled, unsure of my humour. 'We're an escape room, have you been to one before?'

I shook my head and looked at the indiscernible writing on the walls. I'd heard plenty about them but hadn't visited one before. That was about to change.

For those unfamiliar with this type of business, an Escape Room is basically a themed room (think crystal maze) which you are locked into for exactly one hour and in that time you have to find your way out through a series of clues, locks and secret doors with the timer reaching a crescendo as the hour strikes one. If you don't escape within the allotted 60 minutes then a big gaping maw opens up in the floor and you are cast down into the bowels of hell, to burn for a thousand eternities without tapas or even a cooled Cana for company (a slight exaggeration in the last part but you get the general idea).

The blonde beside me sighed "Me and my partner have loved creating this business but have decided to sell up as we have other things to run in Marbella and can't find the time to do them both unfortunately. If you know of anyone that's interested in buying... a couple could run it quite easily between them..."

Sprinting excitedly back to the flat, trolley devoid of E numbers, I breathlessly inform my husband what I had found nestled only 3 streets away and he listens with mounting excitement. Without pause for thought we run back up the road to check out the locked rooms and then we are shown the financial books on the business. My husband's eyes meet mine and I know he has fallen in love.

Within 7 days we had managed to borrow €4K for the deposit and arranged to take over the rooms in our names once the money for our already sold apartment was nestled in the bank. Until that day arrived we were allowed onto the premises to get the place ready for the forthcoming Easter Trade. Eager hands were shook and keys and cash were exchanged and lives were altered, all because I took a detour on my quest for replenished Bimbo.

Hundreds of hours we spent redecorating the rooms, adding new enigmas and updating the old. My husband was in his electrical element, all thoughts of the Salon Varieties and their unwarranted redundancy long gone. Doors opened magically and our imagination ran riot.
I no longer had to apply for jobs that I knew deep down I wouldn't stick too. We were going to work for ourselves, immersed in a world that was a mixture of theatre and mystery and hopefully, profit.
Life was good. We'd found our slice of utopia. For us, an escape was needed no more. The sale of the flat was almost complete and we had started taking future bookings and then...

... And then covid happened.

Our dream is disintegrating along with Spanish tourism. The world is closing its doors and the Earth's normality is shattering. Bars lie empty, mannequins stand inert and freedom of movement is nothoing but yesterday's memory.

So with heavy hearts and with imminent rent to pay we have no choice but to walk away. The day we are finally allowed back out into society, for an early morning masked walk, the keys we will reluctantly have hand back and lose that 4K, but better that than the shirts off our backs. Until that day arrives we will join the rest of the world on the sofa, unemployed and awaiting confirmation from a series of men in suits scattered across the globe who promise that normality will resume again 'one day soon'.

This is it, 'the new normal'. Boris has just announced that everyone who visits Spain must quarantine for 14 days once back in the UK. This will leave millions of people unemployed here once again, businesses once thriving will lie empty, lives shattered, bank accounts devoid of funds, all because of a few outbreaks in Catalonia.

We who live here can go back outdoors as long as masks are worn. They've become the new 'must have' accessory. Handbags and heels are so last year, not unlike the Brits foreign holidays.

So I guess for now, our dreams haven't ended, they are just taking a Covid detour.

DAY.. NIGHT...
WHO KNOWS?

Isolation Lessons Learned

1. Don't try and pretend that the man behind you in the supermarket isn't your husband. The security guard has watched you argue all the way up the street and is well aware that you are daring to shop together. Yelling 'my backs gone and I can't carry the Cruzcampo alone' won't stop him from throwing you and your old lady trolly out into the street while your spouse continues to hunt for the elusive vintage cheddar while oblivious of your departure, safely wandering alone on aisle three.

2. Don't try to move apartment whilst on lock down. Hurling your belongings commando style into a white transit at the crack of dawn isn't fun. Yelling 'go go go' every time the road is clear of ambling oldies makes you feel like you are stealing your own possessions. Trying to get permission from the police to relocate is akin to juggling snakes in a vat of jelly.

3. Eating 11 Easter eggs because 'they were on offer in iceland' isn't the best way to approach your bikini body. Summer will arrive at some point even though lock down appears to have obliterated the sun's rays along with your common sense and easy going attitude.

4. Don't try and be 'strong' all the time. It's ok to yell 'When this is over I'm leaving you ALL and moving to Tobago/Wigan/

Minnesota on my own!!' They know you don't really mean it because let's be honest, you'll have f*ck all left in the bank when that time comes so you'll just have to exist in simmering silence until either covid 19 bumps you off or you get type 2 diabetes from all the shit you've eaten in the past 3 months.

5. Don't try and rent your canine out to strangers to earn another income. Cowdogs are pretty easy to spot.

6. When the take aways finally reopen for collection, kebab isn't ok to eat every other day just because it comes with a salad. Nor is fine to let your husband order a curry online then spend the next 5 days shaking your head at him because he ordered incorrectly and your still eating the 30 onion bhajis costing the same price as your first car as he pressed the 0 by mistake.

7. Realising that 3 months has passed and you still haven't written the novel people keep saying you should write. You finally discover it's not that you don't have the time, it's because you just can't be arsed.

8. Deciding to have an 8pm walk along the seafront and bumping into an old friend doesn't allow you to sit down on separate benches for a quick catch up because you will suddenly be surrounded by 5 police men on motorbikes who ask you to stand up against the wall while they yell 'Are you sitting or walking?? Sitting or walking??' Whilst taking your ID and making you feel like a drug dealer as opposed to a normal human being who just wanted to say hello to a friend you hadn't seen in months.

9. Staring at the communal pool won't make it open any quicker; nor will it enable you to swim like Sharon Davis when you finally get into it.

10. When life finally transcends into the new normal it's ok to do bugger all some days. It's fine to binge watch Killing Eve and plan your new career as a middle aged assassin just as long as

you don't have to get up too early. You won't get arrested if the washing up isn't done at night or if you decide to wear your nightdress to walk the dog. It's ok to be human and to fail and to be weak and to shout and miss your family. It's ok to be you.

I've had enough, I'm going crazy
I've become the epitome of lazy
I can't go out, I can't walk free
I'm starting to resemble a 4th Bee Gee

My thighs they chafe, my hairs all grey
I'm expanding rapidly day by day
My back is f*cked from sitting down
Becoming one with my dressing gown

The virus is here, of that we're sure
We watch 'This Morning' and await a cure
My brain unemployed like most of Spain
Ambition and dreams washed down the drain

So hear my plea and let us out
Before my marriage goes up the spout
I'll risk my life against Wuhan
If you'll just remove this feckin Ban!

PHASE 3... YIPPEE!

We've moved!

"It's not going to open up any quicker by you staring at it day in day out."

Ignoring the middle aged voice behind me I look longingly at the enticing cool blue water rippling in the sunlight beneath me. Swaying palm trees complete the oasis and I sigh out loud, brushing at the sweat forming on my brow.

"900 euros", I mutter under my breath "900 euros a month for a rental apartment we can only use as a pretty prison."

I stand on my tiptoes and squint over the boundary at my agile neighbours in their lycra wear, jumping gleefully into their 'monitored' wet and wild wonderland and I can feel the injustice of it all encase me like an unwelcome shroud.

"Look over there Marcus, they are allowed in their communal pool so why aren't we?"

I petulantly kick at one of Brian's tennis balls which promptly hits a plant pot and swiftly richochets over the wall onto the tendered green below. Brian, who is under the misguided assumption that he is the canine offspring of Peter Parker proceeds to scale the wall in persuit of his favourite toy but promptly forgets his rescue mission after he spots a few stray ginger nut crumbs nestling underneath the wilting Aloe Vera.

'Well I'm contacting the owner's son , he's already made us pay an extra 270 euros as a penalty because we couldn't move in on the day he wanted us to during lock down PLUS he's got two months deposit, a months rent and the months agency fee. We could have had 2 weeks at Universal Studios for that price plus all the Butter Beer we could stomach in Diagon alley.

I can feel my last few apathetic hormones bristling internally at the insanity of it all. Come back 2019, all is forgiven.

"Worse things happen mum, people are rioting all over London," yells an online schooled voice, "Can I have some cereal?"
"I told you to get it before the class started," I shout back into the makeshift Covid classroom.

Any voice of reason is not welcome when I'm having a full on meltdown and I stomp back into the lounge to throw myself into the arms of Piers 'ranty' Morgan for an hour.

As a fully-fledged control freak I'm finding communicating with the Spanish landlord's son an arduous task. On moving into the rental apartment we had anticipated and agreed upon the removal and disposal of a giant piece of mahogany furniture which resembled something from Mr Sowerbury's parlor blocking 90% of the sunlight from the lounge. On arrival this monstrosity was still firmly in situ so we had to spend the next 3 days dismantling it and painting the bright yellow wall behind it. Also 2 large padlocks held the patio doors closed and the old lady who owned the flat didn't have a clue where the keys were so they had to be drilled off before we could breathe in the outside air.

"Do you want to go across the road to the pub for lunch? He's got Stroganoff on today?"

I lower my chin and shake my head. I'd eaten enough food this year to carry me into 2021. My birthday had been the previous week and I had celebrated my 53rd year by trying to give myself gout from consuming the 3 birthday cakes that friends had brought over to celebrate the fact we were allowed back into each other's homes and lives.

Peeling my bottom lip off the sofa I reluctantly wander out into the hallway only to see a piece of paper being slipped under the front door. Bending creakily down to pick it up I gaze blankly at the Spanish writing adorning the crisp white sheet and my mouth suddenly drops. Certain words jump out at me and the blood that has been slowly simmering all morning reaches boiling point.

"Don't go making any plans this Thursday evening," I yell to the coffee-preparing adult form in the kitchen, "there's a meeting taking place by the 'terminally redundant' pool for all the residents. Apparently they are going to decide whether the pool can open again... THIS YEAR!!!!" [*Insert Maniacal Laughter*]

With shaking hands I place the slip of paper on the sideboard and walk back out onto the balcony.

"I'm going in that bloody pool this weekend, come hell or high water. The cocoon brigade can go take up residence elsewhere. Neptune's apprentice ain't for turning."

THE NEW NORMAL.

"**Y**ou're going to break that keyboard if you bang it any harder, I thought we were going down to the pool that you so desperately wanted open? Are you listening? Get off bloody Facebook!"

I hold my fingers up to silence my husband as I'm currently in an online argument with an affluent pensioner (seated no doubt in their mortgage free ivory tower) who is insistent that we are all better off without tourism.

We spent the vast majority of our savings on buying the flat as my husband did have a job, a contracted one at the Salon Varietes Theatre and was beyond excited to have the career of his dreams and a regular income here but as you well know, sometimes our happy slumber turns into a world without light and almost one year later to the day, through no fault of his own he was made redundant and was forced to exit stage left.

This series of events sent my husband into a downward spiral, a feeling many are experiencing now, and he would spend days in bed and unable to face the world, the breadwinner without a crust to feed us.

Now as you know I'm a Northerner, my bedside manner leaves a lot to be desired. Nurse Ratchet looks like Florence Nightingale in comparison. My knee jerk reaction was to yell 'get up, get out, get on with it' which probably didn't help nor gain me any future foot rubs; but after a week of my banging the mop against the door and playing Guns & Roses at full volume, he finally arose, bearded, jaded and in the need of a pint of Nescafé.

As a fully qualified electrical technician in the UK (electrical estimator and project manager, I stand corrected) he dusted off his pliars and resumed the work he'd left behind 20 years ago along with the grey skies and life went on.

I attempted to add butter to the Warburtons whenever the opportunity arose but with our meagre savings obliterated, we had no choice but to sell our home and move into rented accommodation. But life goes on...that was yesterday's news.

So here we are, almost a 100 days on from day one of isolation, a 'new' normal is upon the horizon. The government has tried to keep our heads above sea level, all of us under pension age treading water until tourism resumes and our *new life in the sun* can resume, mine included.

A voice breaks through my reverie. "Are you coming for a swim or not? I'm stood here like a right twat in my Speedo's. Oh and the sparrows you keep feeding have multiplied are all sat on the oven waiting for breakfast. There was 5 at last count. One was sat on Brian's head chirping away, I don't think he even noticed to be fair, too busy wondering if he could blend into the feathered ensemble."

I close the laptop and look up at the blue sky. Today is Monday the 22nd of June and tourism has been allowed to resume, albeit tentatively for the economy, it has no choice but to do so.

Holiday makers with factor 50 will return because everyone wants and deserves some sunshine in their lives. The local bar owners will dust off their shutters (but only if the landlords have been understanding with a reduced rent) and will happily pour you a larger than average measure with a relieved smile. Hotels will sweep away the dust sheets and shops will awaken their tills with a flourish and assistants will iron out the creases on the mannequins as life resumes its *new normal*.

But...all this is only possible if you return to us. Climb down from your mountain top retreats and spend a bit of your hard earned pension on a tapas or two. Fly the skies in your masks and sit on our beaches at a respectable distance. Don't let this horrendous virus dictate your lives.

I stretch my arms and yawn. My husband has grown tired of waiting and has fallen asleep on the sofa, towel wrapped around his tanned waist. A female sparrow suddenly flies into the lounge and lands on the coffee table, looking at me with motherly impatience.

"Ok, ok I'm coming. You have mouths to feed too" and I arise with my tiny companion, one on foot, the other on wings, both trying to ensue their family is fed; all of us trying to do our best in this uncertain world.

DIVING MISS DAISY

"**G**et your trunks and sun cream on we're going out! I've had enough of the urine infested community pool, it's time to head into deeper waters!

Two sets of eyes look up from the sofa but bottoms remain firmly attached to the Draylon. Top Gear is in full swing. What could possibly compete with watching 3 Middle Aged men with thinning hair cavort through France on a supermarket trolly in a race to buy the last buttered croissant?

"We're going scuba diving!!" I yell, trying to invoke some excitement into the immobile forms in front of me.

"We've not done that for over 4 years madre" my son sighs. "Do they actually have wetsuits big enough to fit you now you've expanded? We'll have to do a refresher course or dad will have a panic attack again"

"That water was bloody cold, it was just a sodding shock that's all! I'm not as confident as you two are. Your forgetting that my dad wasn't the man from Atlantis like yours Paula!" The elder male yells all this as he storms off to find more digestives. The door slams dramatically behind him.

I sigh, smile through gritted teeth and raise my voice so I can be heard throughout the newly painted rental.

"We're going to have a nice family day out whether you like it or not without the need for telephones or TV's or PlayStations. Now if you would all be so kind as to get your bloody swimwear on forthwith or I will personally rip every plug off every device and hurl them out the window! I'll be waiting in the car. Don't forget your masks!!"

Two hours later we are all huddled round a mini bus listening to a no nonesence northern lady explaining how best to breathe under water without the aid of gills. There are 6 of us in total, the other 3 comprise of a Scottish father and son whose accent is so strong that we all just smile and nod whenever he poses a question and behind him loiters a supermodel from Hawaii. I shuffle away from the stunning creature and place myself between the instructor and my set of tanks and listen to the instructions on how not to die and what not to touch.

Wet suits are handed out and we all gingerly place our feet inside. Closing my eyes I drag the ensemble over my hips and suck my stomach in as much as my non-existent muscles allow. Jiggling my torso I inch it up until the zip is in place and I hastily tug it up around my shoulders and squeeze my bingo wings into the second skin. Encouraged by my own ability to not have fallen over In the process, I catch sight of myself in the rear view mirror and i stop mid smile and stare at the apparition before me. A pregnant seal in a scrunchie. Behind me the 'Hawain Princess' glides by in a suit the size of my left thigh and bends over to put her boots on. I can feel beads of perspiration begin to form.

"Marcus... MARCUS! You're going to help me get my footwear on, I can't reach my feet!!"

My husband isn't listening, he's too busy admiring himself in the window of a parked car. He's the only person on Earth to have lost weight during the pandemic and I can mentally hear him mumble *'how YOU doing?'* as he strokes his flat torso ensconced in the man made skin. I poke him unceremoniously in the back.

"Will you stop preening and help me get these sodding boots on!" Sweat is dripping down my back and I can feel the anxiety of middle age creeping in.
My son is already suited up and jumping off rocks into the sea with the instructors assistant. I smile inwardly as I see the Scots attempting the highland fling whilst wriggling into their suits and I breathe deeply and await the final instructions.

"Right everyone, let's get those tanks on your backs, make sure you all check your buddy out. No going off on your own, make sure your partner is next to you. We'll split into two groups"

I look pointedly at my son who mouths 'what?' I know once he's in the sea he will suddenly become Aquaman, diving in and out of every nook and cranny in search of the elusive Kraken without a thought for the person floundering without oxygen beside him.

The sea looks like an infinite stretch of blue glass and I stagger to the waters edge like an ancient turtle sporting a metal shell. On command I inflate my buoyancy device and place my mouthpiece in. Inhaling the oxygen into my mouth i remind myself not to breathe through my nose. A peacefulness envelopes me and I give the hand gesture that everything is fine.

Slowly we deflate the air on our shoulders and our multi-shaped bodies slip down under the water, size no longer matters as we become one with the fishes.

All the noise from the tourists on the shore become non-existent and the world which we try so hard to control slips away from our grasp as a new universe begins. Multicoloured fish pass by our goggles without fear or apprehension, accepting these flippered interlopers as one of their own. Gliding through the depths I suddenly remember how much I love this activity. My husband points at the seabed as an octopus propels itself through a bed of rocks. My son is ahead of me, steaming though the water like a silky seal. My body is weightless and I greedily look around at what nature has managed to keep sacred for millions of years.

The instructor gestures us all to pass through two caverns in single file and I stay happily at the back, confident in my ability to manoeuvre my ample buttocks through the crevice. I kick my heels like an underwater Dorothy and I feel something slip out from behind me. Stopping in my tracks I turn to see something sat on the sea bed. It's blue. It looks like a flipper. Someone's lost a flipper. I shake my head in amazement. Who could be so silly as to lose a flipper and not notice it had gone. I turn back and struggle down to retrieve it from the seabed. Grabbing it I turn to swim back up to join my companions but I don't appear to be moving. I kick my legs again but stay sat immobile on the seabed. Suddenly I realise my I'm going nowhere. The missing flipper is mine.

WATER WAY TO GO

So here I am, all 53 years of me, loitering on the seabed awaiting my unplanned watery demise.

I try not to breathe too heavily as I am fully aware how rapidly the oxygen in my tank can deplete if panic sets in. At least I won't have to worry about what to cook for tea tonight if this the final exit as I shuffle off this mortal coil. I will undoubtedly become useful as future fish fodder or, as time passes, a shark's toothpick. Peacefulness settles over me as I sway alongside the Sea Anemones.

Closing my eyes I think back to all the wonderful things I have done in life and smile inwardly at the famous people I have met on my travels around the globe.

The young actor I lived (and cavorted) with back in the early 90's who went on to become 'The Master' of his trade after I unceremoniously dumped him at drama school as I was too young, stupid and egotistical to live in his ever expanding shadow.

The vest-wearing big screen action hero of the 90's, who decided he fancied a bit of karaoke whilst promoting his chain of restaurants in Hong Kong, who happened upon our dimly lit karaoke bar and then took it upon himself to invite a cascade of eager young waitresses back to his hotel to indulge in song, champagne and a couple of strange smelling cigarettes. Sitting in the shadows listening to the conversation I marveled how he remembered all these star struck female's names and then, noticing my reluctance to partake in the hand rolled unfiltered, offered to blow the smoke from his mouth into mine whilst patting the seat invitingly beside him.

The Asian Kung-fu master I strolled arm in arm with down a never ending staircase, laughing theatrically until the director finally shouted 'CUT' when finally our painted smiles could morph into genuine ones. Silks and finery cast aside, he sat across from me on the floor eating dim sum whilst talking animatedly about how he missed his family and encouraged me to open up about my own travels and experiences along the way. After chopsticks were placed on empty bowls he shook my hand and bid me farewell as the pre-booked mini bus returned me to the other side of the island to the notorious 16th floor in Chunking Mansions and back to my jaded reality.

Slouching on the stern of a famous Jockeys yacht and attempting to act sober whilst throwing up the previous night's tequila whenever he turned his back to pour us yet another glass of wine. Then to cap it all, falling ungracefully overboard into the shallow sea when my attempts to wipe off stray vomit from a glistening Jet Ski was rudely interrupted by a kamikaze seagull.

Being picked up in a limo by a very wealthy Asian hotelier, clad in my finest 'Dolfe&Guarana' only to be whisked off to a 'Pay per hour' hotel room which was encased in floor to ceiling wipe down pleather. Needless to say his happy ending never occurred and I marched my stupidly naïve self and my gravity defying stilettos off to the nearest Golden Arches where I treated me and my fragile ego to several items on the menu, washed down with a full fat cok (their spelling not mine)

Chatting quietly to Steve Pemberton about past episodes of Inside Number 9 whilst our eight year old boys ran amok inside stationary trains being used for the filming of the final scenes of Mapp & Lucia. The conversation unfortunately was cut short with the arrival of Miranda Richardson yelling as to the whereabouts of her teeth and the fact that her tuna had been fiddled with.

A gentle tap on my goggles brings me back to the present day. Two glass-encased blue eyes look enquiringly into my own.

Whilst engrossed in my reverie the instructor had kindly replaced the flipper onto my foot and was giving me the signal to continue with the dive. Kicking my heels I leave a cloud of sand in my wake as I streamline my way back into the group who had scarcely noticed I had gone.

Looking around at the multi-coloured underwater utopia I realize how lucky we are to be able to have the freedom to have this adventure under the sea, even if we are temporarily unable to have anything similar on land.

I immediately make a promise to myself. From now on I am going to look forward and not back, Covid-19 will eventually end and the opportunity to create unforgettable memories will begin again. The world will open its creaking doors to all of us who are not afraid to walk through them and freedom will resume! (Apart from all of you who voted to leave the E.U. You should from this day forth be forced to eat only Poundland beans whilst camping in Skegness in February).

EPILOGUE

The 12 Days of Shitfest

Christmas? Bah humbug!

1. Sneaking into Mijas Iceland when you live in Fuengirola during the municipality lock down; you know it's not allowed. There are trained snipers on the bridge, awaiting your departure, the sightline focused of your ever inflating torso. You are a warrior clad in elasticated pants and your desire for a Warburton's toasted crumpet is greater than your need to ever see the grandchildren again. They can visit you in

prison, be a day out for them. No one comes between you and a hot buttered hole.

2. You look like Ken Dodd. Your hairdresser isn't sure if she's allowed to work or not due the constantly revised rules so you've taken upon yourself to embrace the grey. The silver weeds start to push up through the fake chestnut brown and you stare at the vintage white stripe and your mother's eyes in the mirror. Cautiously you look down to see if the cuffs match the collar but all you can see is your pasty wobbling stomach. You sigh and head to the kitchen for your 7th digestive of the morning.

3. You spend hours before daylight plotting how to kill off your snoring spouse and ponder if anyone has ever actually farted themselves to death.

4. You find yourself yelling 'FUCK!' a lot as you close the front door behind you, realizing a second too late that the 8 inches of elasticized nylon isn't adorning your ears.

5. You suddenly become religious, praying that the school stays open because you can't even be bothered to brush your teeth never mind self-educate the fruit of your loins and, let's be honest; Judge Rinder is on in 10 minutes.

6. You watch the BBC news daily and shake your head at the imbeciles in the U.K. Parliament spouting crap without a mask. Brexit and Covid, Covid and Brexit. It's the new Morecambe & Wise, minus a punch line.

7. Face book has become your new best friend, and eternal enemy. It makes you mean. You sit in gleeful anticipation, awaiting the next stupid question to appear on your favorite expat forum. Questions that have been asked a thousand times before are mocked by the bored and the restless. We are smug, we live here, you voted to leave the EU; you wallow in the damp

consequences of your actions.

8. You stop making eye contact with people when outside. There's no point anymore. Babies in prams look up at their parents faces, disguised parental smiles hidden by masks are not reciprocated by the new Covid generation. Are teeth even mandatory anymore? Dentists go out of business alongside lipstick manufacturers.

9. My jeans no longer zip up, my bra cup runneth over but thankfully a wayward custard cream still manages to fit in my mouth.

10. You look back at old holiday photos and long for the day your flight is delayed for a few hours and not a few months. Your parents back in the U.K. say they are ok but you can hear the worry in their voices. Covid has robbed us all of our humour and replaced it with fear and uncertainty. We send presents home for Christmas and stare vacantly as fairy lights twinkle half-heartedly in stores without conviction or audience.

11. We venture out to our favourite bar but it's closed down. I peer through the window at empty tables and cloth covered chairs. Dust bunnies cascade across the customer less floor. Spain hasn't been kind to the self employed. We are cast aside like yesterday's tapas. Friends & colleagues return back to the U.K., tills no longer ringing, with false smiles and heavy hearts they lean into the arms of their family leaving behind only shattered dreams of their new life in the sun.

12. We have a vaccine. It may be full of micro chips or fish and chips, who knows, not I. My PHD is still in the post. Will I take it? Certainly! I have to admit I put more crap into my body in the 90's than one small prick could ever contain. I look at my phone, its 9.55am on Christmas Eve. The presents are wrapped and Brian the ever hopeful is looking at me with a full bladder. My son and husband are asleep in their beds and the sun is shining outside. I pull on my big girl pants and catch sight of myself

in the Mirror. A little chubbier with a few more lines than this time last year, but I'm alive, and I have Vodka and a roof over my head. So from me to you, have as much of a Merry Christmas as you can, smile at strangers through your masks even though they can't see your lips and always look up to the blue sky and not the grey pavement below and remember, roast bat will never be on a civilized worlds Christmas menu, no matter how much they charge for a turkey crown in Iceland.

AND NOW FOR SOMETHING COMPLETELY DIFFERENT

Before we moved to the Costa Del Sol we visited several regions of Spain in our quest to find our little corner of utopia.

It was on one of these long car journeys that the conversation turned to fictional characters from fairy tales that, given the choice, we would chose to become. My husband remarked that Robin Hood always seemed to be having fun with his merry men pillaging in the forest and I replied that I'd change places with Snow White as with seven chaps in the house the bin was bound to get taken out and shelves put up with good humour and a song.

My eyelids started to grow heavy. I dozed off pondering how Cinderella was coping with her middle aged spread and if the magic mushrooms of the forest made a suitable substitute for

HRT. On that note, with the rolling mountains by my side, the following short scripted story was born.

HAPPILY EVER
AFTER..?

by Paula Leskovitz
(Image by Graham Spencer Photography)

(*Empty room. Few posters.*)

<u>A church hall</u>
Snow White is sat on a mat attaching her HRT patch. She is in her full Snow White ensemble. Stretching (warming up), she notices the audience

SNOW
(*To audience*) Have u come for the class? Yes me too. thought I'd give is a whirl, I'm not getting very far with weight watchers... Every time I lose a few lbs I celebrate by having a Twix. Can you believe back in the day I used to have a waist the size of a pogo stick but since I hit the big 50 even looking at a quaver makes me put on 7lbs. I literally went to bed one night all lithe and moist after a particularly enjoyable episode of Mad Men and woke up two sizes bigger, paddling in a pool of sweat!
And heck knows where my libidos gone... I feel like an alien in my own body....Oh speaking of oddities... Here she comes... The resident cat lady of tarnished town.

(*Sneezing is heard. Cruella enters. Head to foot in Cruella gear. Glam. Posh. Neurotic. Not as slim as she used to be*)

CRUELLA
I swear to god if Rumpulstiltskin lets those bloody dogs out again at 4am I'll shove his head so hard onto that spinning wheel he'll have that spun gold coming out of his Arse for months. (*Rolls her mat out and takes some Valium out of her fur bag and tips them into her mouth straight from the bottle*)

SNOW
'Morning CRU. How's your pussy?

CRUELLA
(*Taking the tablets*) Oh darling she's been up all night mewling at the moon. I think she must be 'with kitty'. I'll bet my last pair of Christian Laboutins she's been frolicking with Cinders Tabby. I'm telling you it will be like an episode of gremlins... those kittens will 'pop' out like the united colours of Benetton I just know it! And her a Pure breed Persian blue... What will the neighbours think?

(*A Man all in green rushes in. Thick glasses. Holding a bow and arrow. Goes straight up to CRU... In her face*)

ROBIN
'Are you here for the speed awareness course? '(*Looks around suspiciously... Pointing his bow*)

CRUELLA
'No I'm certainly not.

ROBIN
Oh right. AA??

CRUELLA
Do I look like a woman that wants to give up the last solitary pleasure in life for sobriety?

ROBIN
Dwarf rehabilitation?

CRU
NO!!

ROBIN
Ok ok, keep your fur on. What is going on in here then??

SNOW (*points to the sign*) 'Charming Yoga'

(*The door bangs. Lumiere walks in. He's put on a few lbs since his film debut. Candelabra in each hand*)

LUMIERE
(*French*) 'Ello

(*Robin walks up to him. Very close. Looks him up and down*)

ROBIN
Didn't I pilfer you from beauty and the beasts castle and donate you to the little old lady who lived in a shoe to brighten her place up? Bloody hell, you've put on a bit of pork since I last saw you, too many sausage rolls and not enough pillaging methinks.

LUM (*looks him up & down*)
Oh ho ho, I never knew that the jolly green giant was so short and lacking in personality (*sniffs*) what's that smell? Ah, the well known fragrance of 'au de damp moss'. And you wonder why Marion left you...

(*Robin raises his bow and aims it at Lum. At that moment Prince Charming walks in, in full Lycra splendour and camp as christmas*)

CHARMING
Hello girls... Sorry I'm late, I had a run in with Cinders at the bus stop, and she's still soooo bitter. Hips the size of sandbags. I said is it any wonder I swapped sides after the seventh child. I mean, we're still friends, I even offered to get her vaginal rinoplasy for her birthday but apparently, having never regions like a battered tulip is all the rage!! ' Right Mats out!!!

(Robin tries to get on snows mat and she pushes him off)

(Running in is a woman, slightly out of breath. Clutching Dunkin' Donuts. Weary. Narcoleptic)

SLEEPING BEAUTY
Sorry sorry sorry. I slept in.

CHARMIMNG
That's no excuse Miss Beauty, you've had more sleep than I've had wild nights out with one direction. Let's be honest, even when that gorgeous princely hunk tried to snog your face off in a vain attempt to raise you from your slumber you carried on snoozing.... When that stud muffin tried to bring you round with loves first kiss...

SNOW
... Erm.... that was me actually... I got loves first kiss

CHARMING
Was it? Oh I get you all mixed up what with your taffeta frocks, power naps and 80's hairdo's. Anyway, Beauty wasn't having any of it. Out like a light! He ended up having to waft a family tub of Haagen Dazs under her 'shnoz' to wake her up! Poor Princy P had to have therapy afterwards, Confidence annihilated. Shame he didn't smear peanut butter all over his lips first...that would have roused you.
(Walking away) and they wonder why there are no decent straight men left around...

(BEAUTY looks down at her do nuts and takes a reproachful bite)

BEAUTY
If you'd been asleep for the last 10 years you'd be slightly peckish too! Anyway... Prince or no prince, he reeked of garlic and hadn't even bothered to shave. *(To snow)*
He may have been his type... but he certainly wasn't mine *(shudders)*
Anyway, Where's Rapunzel today. Isn't she coming?

SNOW
Letting down her hair.., AGAIN! She went out last night with sleepy dozy and doc. They introduced her to the magic mushrooms of the forest. Last time I saw her she was staggering round the woods trying to slay the dragon with her GHD hair straighteners and a can of Elnette. Heck... Is it hot in here or is it me??
(Wafts herself)

BEAUTY *(fingers a do nut and eats it while rolling out her mat.)*
I didn't actually mind being in that deep sleep. No stress, no weight gain, no Nigel Farage, no worrying about what to cook for dinner. Since I've woken up I've gone right off men. I've had enough pricks in my hand to last a lifetime

ROBIN
No shit Sherwood...

SNOW
Oh I couldn't agree more, I mean how much poison can you inject into a vanilla toffee triple choc muffin?? That Apple was almost the death of me! I tried bananas but we didn't get on... Brought me out in hives.

PRINCE
OK!! Right my little pot bellied piggies its time to get bendy!!

(Everyone, who is yet to, rolls their mats out and gets into position)

LUMINIERE *(to snow)*
I can only do the downward dog. I almost lost a candle when I attempted the crab. The hospital said they were refusing to remove anymore in A&E and I'd have to go private next time. I wouldn't have minded but the big bad wolf was in the next bed to me and we were down to one nurse by the time they'd reattached my wick. No wonder the NHS is on its knees. All the nurses have been eaten.

ROBIN
Anyone got a spare mat?

EVERYONE NO!

(Robin leaves and comes back in with a piece of Astroturf)

CHARMING
Ok... *(Starts doing Yoga moves)*
'Right ladies, those pelvic floors need to get tightened or you'll be single

FOREVER!!
(To BEAUTY)
Miss sleepy head, you left a moist reminder on my tongue and groove last time you were here, which even my Mr muscle wouldn't budge so.. Get clenching!

(BEAUTY *looks embarrassed and takes another bite of the do-nut and sulks*)

ROBIN *(to CRU)*
I'd like to tongue and groove you, you foxy minx.

CRU   Get away
from me you grime encrusted letch. One step closer and you'll leave me with no choice *(gets out weed killer from her back and threatens him with it)* I'd rather adopt an alligator as a pet than have you anywhere near my sacred garden

(Robin sidles over to SB)

BEAUTY
'Dream on moss boy'

(Robin goes back to his Astro Turf, muttering, and they get into position)

LUM
I blame LED lighting *(to no one in particular)* One day everyone wants the flickering glow of candlelight the next they are twiddling with their knobs dimming every room at the press of a button. I've not sat at a table for months...

ROBIN
Any bloody wonder; they'd be no room for the food with your fat arse on there.

SLEEPING
I once went to dinner at Beauty and the Beasts place. Got my best George at Asda frock on and everything, sat there all night listening to his tales about how beauty came from within. Every time I Reached out for a vol-au-vent it skipped off the plate and started dancing with the silverware. I was so hungry I ended up decapitating a scotch egg as it waltzed by with a crème brûlée. I shoved it in my trap before anyone realised it was missing from the final walk-down. Good job I had a few dusty peanut treats hiding in the bottom of my handbag or I swear I would have passed out!

CRU

Food is soooo overrated dahhling. A large G+T followed by a Probiotic chaser is all I need to get me through the day. I've not touched carbs since that sordid incident when the dish ran away with the spoon back in 1963

ROBIN

I prefer a bit of meat with my gravy. Some junk in the trunk!! My Marion used to have a bottom like a Waitrose trifle... *(Starts to weep)*

CRU

I don't know whether to be more surprised to know that someone was ever foolish enough to have sex with you voluntarily... or that you've actually shopped at Waitrose.

LUM

I used to love a browse round LIDL. I was always in there on a Saturday sniffing the Brie...then they introduced the 'middle aisle'... You know, the aisle of stuff we don't really need but it's like a field off poppies... Your drawn to it with no idea why your there. I'd just be popping in to see if there were any chocolate marzipan logs on offer and come out with a towel heater and a leopard print Mankini. To this day I've still not mounted that towel heater.

BEAUTY

I get mine delivered now. So much easier. You don't even have to leave the sofa. I like to watch 'this morning' with a gypsy cream. That Philip Schofield is such a Fox. It's not the same mind you since Fern left the show. I remember her final words on the chaise lounge before she sauntered off hand in hand with Phil Vicary.
'It's not a gastric band viewers, it's eating healthy that's made me so thin'
Pfffff.... Then next time you see her she's four sizes smaller and promoting ready meals for pensioners with Ronnie Corbet!
She was proper woman shaped back in the day. Have you seen her recently? She's got a neck like a turtle and shops in New look as opposed to EVANS. I mean really, what's the point of having a flat stomach if your boobs look like they are in a race to join your feet? Laughs... *(Falls asleep)*

ROBIN

(weeping)
I used to cook cock au van for Marion. She loved my slow roasted free

range beef with garlic crusted potatoes. Now she's decided to become a vegan and lives her life foraging in the forest with another woman who has thighs bigger than Gaston's. I tried to win her back with some lightly fried lardons but she was having none of it. How can I compete with tofu? Who the fuck eats tofu? You can't even use it for grouting your tent.

SNOW

Their their...You can't change the past. You have to move on. When my husband walked out I thought my life had ended. But you just get on with it, you don't have any choice. Then when my first born Kevin wanted to move to London to work for Coutts bank I thought my heart would break! My only boy a banker!!
Then the triplets tell me they want to flee the nest on their 18th birthday & travel the world! What can you do? I can't say 'no, stay here and help me write some new harmonies for HI HO!!'
So now all three girls are floating around the med on the ORIANA earning their keep by stripping off other people's soiled bed linen and cleaning toilets. But it's their choice. What can I do?
The dwarfs all have their own lives too, granted three of them are currently in rehab but you have to find something to do to ease the pain of the empty nest. I spent the best years of my life bringing them all up and without blowing my own trumpet; I think I've done a bloody good job. *(Looks down at her hands)*

(Everyone is quiet)

CHARMING

Is this a bloody Yoga class or an episode of the Jeremy Kyle show?? *(Beauty wakes)* I swear I'm going to cancel all your wedding invites if you embarrass me by turning up in anything above a size 12! Elton has promised to sing a few numbers and I won't have my day ruined by you staining his Versace suit with your sob stories. Get those hips off the ground and straddle that mat. I want to hear those bones crack!

CRU

(Quietly) How dare he. I've never been a size 12 in my life.

LUM

I think my right thigh is a size 12. You'd think being this hot constantly would keep you slim but no. I used to run from restaurants to taverns several times a day, a party wasn't a party without me on their table. Now I'm lucky if I get dragged out at Xmas and that's only because belle has had some more plastic work done and will only sit under a 'flattering light'. I think she sat a bit close to my flame on the last 'date night' because by the time the lamb shank had arrived she looked like one of Salvador Dali's sculptures. Even the beast looked attractive in comparison.

(*Snow changers the subject to lighten the mood*)

SNOW
So are you working at all now beauty?

BEAUTY
(*Embarrassed*) Actually I've just got a new job.

CRU
Oh how vulgar. Even the word Employment makes me feel quite faint. I tried it once. Didn't like it. An hour for lunch? Who does lunch in an hour? It takes me that long to choose what I'm going to order then to not eat it!
That's why I breed pussies. They see to themselves and don't make you clock in and out.

SNOW (*looks at BEAUTY*)
Ignore her. Go on. What is it?

BEAUTY
Well.... I was watching a programme about people who 'get off' on watching people eat.

ROBIN
Get off? How?

BEAUTY
Well... They sit in their marks and Spencer's undies and eat food and people pay to watch them... You know... Watch them eat?

ROBIN
Why the hell would anyone pay to watch people eat in their undies? You can go to Benidorm and sit in McDonald's and do that for free! Loads of fat fuckers there stuffing their faces wearing bikinis 4 sizes too small!

BEAUTY
I talk to them too... About their lives and their kids and even what their favourite ice cream is. Mines pistachio. So sometimes we share a bowl of frozen dessert together online...and...

CRU
And?

BEAUTY
(Small voice) And sometimes we play hide & seek with the flake.

LUM
(Lights flicker)

ROBIN
(drops his bow)

CRU
(has a drink from her hip flask)

SNOW
Well that sounds ... Erm... Interesting. I guess you didn't find that advertised in the Observer.

BEAUTY
No, Friday Ad actually. To be honest I really enjoy it. A chap the other day just wanted to sit in silence eating wagon wheels while wearing his mother's tights. Then another dresses up as a dog and I have to feed him chum through the screen while I Jiggle his lead.
So I get paid to eat and chat and even if I fall asleep they stay logged in and just watch me dribble....

CHARMING
... And lift those hips up... Can you feel the burn? Robin stop checking out Cru's Arse and LUM, try and raise your belly off the Mat or you'll never even get that wick reheated.

CRU
(Pause) So let me get this right. Men pay you to eat online while wearing very few clothes and you don't even have to leave the house?

BEAUTY
Yes

CRU
Well that beats working at Superdrug dahhling. Do whatever makes you happy that's my motto. My happy usually involves ice and a slice.

ROBIN
I'm thinking of selling the tent and relocating to a one of those mobile

home things in Crowhurst Park. *(They all look at him)*
They have quite a nice watering hole, loads of tasty wenches serving meat and veg to hungry punters AND they have mead that comes out of a tap!!
Apparently I have to leave the van for a month in January while they close down but that's not a problem, I quite fancy doing an African Safari and little johns just retired so we'll share a jeep and go deer hunting!

LUM
How the hell can you afford all that? I struggle to find the money to get waxed every month?

ROBIN
Lets just say I didn't give everything from the rich to the poor. I'm not getting any younger so I charge a small commission for my services. I'm not a bloody charity! Anyway, I'm getting piles sitting on the damp grass all the time. I quite fancy having hot water occasionally and watching the complete box set of game of thrones on the Axminster with a Chinese take away. There's only so many ways you can BBQ a squirrel.

(Beauty is asleep again)

SNOW
My eldest keeps talking about leaving the banking game and moving to Thailand. He wants to spend a year in a temple with the monks to find himself. I said why can't you find yourself in Morrison's like most of us have to do! I mean London is bad enough, but Thailand! And have you seen those boy ladies? The only way you can tell they were born Derek and not Deirdre is by the Adam's apple. What if they decide to wear a scarf? How could you tell? You could be down the aisle and onto your third slice of marital bliss before you realised your wife pee's standing up.

LUM
I quite fancy taking a cruise. SAGA sent me some brochures the other week. After I got over the shock of being ancient enough to be invited to join the coffin Dodgers I had a browse through them while sat on the loo and to be honest they don't look too bad! I've always fancied seeing the northern lights and it may give me a bit of inspiration. I can't go through life just flickering anymore; I need my embers to burn!!

CHARMING
(Angry) The only thing you lot need to burn in here is a few 100 cal-

ories!! Why do I even bother wasting my time *(leans down to pick up his mat)* I've not seen one abdominal scoop since you sat down on your lazy arses. Oh look beauty has bored herself to sleep again!! *(Someone nudges her awake)* all you do is moan about how fat or bored or uninspired you all are and when I try and help you find your 'happy place' all you is sprawl on the floor and moan more! Well I have better things to do. I have a wedding to organise with cuff links to buy and flowers to arrange so if you don't mind I'll leave you all to your dismal lives and go elsewhere and be FABULOUS on my own!

(Beauty wakes)

BEAUTY
Oh no please don't go!! I'm sorry, we all are *(moves over to charming)* I love coming to these classes. They make me feel 'normal'. What with robin and his chronic BO and lack of any special awareness, Lumiere with his inability to see that unless he moves with the times he'll never be invited to dinner again, snow with her HRT patches and life on hold for her kids, living her life through their eyes, CRU with her denial over eating solids even though I saw her in Nandos only last week covered in chilli sauce and inhaling a chicken wing and then there's me... Using food as an anchor while I drift around in a sea of syrup hoping to find my happy ever in a tub of Haagen Dazs.
(Gently) Don't leave us charming. You are everything we attain to be. You're Happy in your perfectly tanned and toned skin and neon leg warmers. You bounce out of bed every morning and shout 'watch out world... The bitch is up' and never ever apologise for what you are and so that's why I come here, to be a little more charming.

ROBIN
I don't have BO... Do I?

CRU
I was just snorting the chilli flakes.... It's the only legal high I can get nowadays.

SNOW
I do... I have my phone on vibrate all night just in case they need to contact me. And they never do. The only calls I get regularly are from PPI

LUM
that's it... I'm going down Robert Dyas after this. It's low energy

lighting all the way for me from now on. I'll be brighter than Blackpool illuminations on a November evening.

CHARMING

(Looks at them all) well.... Since you pleaded so nicely. Ok, you have one last chance BUT only if you promise to work your backsides as hard as you work your mouths! I could be getting my inside leg measured now at Moss Bross but I'm here instead, getting sweaty in a gloomy hall with the rejects of tarnished town so put some effort in!

(They all lie back down) Charming says 'right... Into the crab!

(Beauty to snow)

BEAUTY

so, what happened to that chap you met on tinder? Last time we spoke you were going to meet him in the slaughtered lamb for a Spritzer?

SNOW

Oh god, it was awful. He looked great on the photo, tall dark and awesome. We chatted on the phone beforehand and he seemed really genuine. So we arrange to meet in the pub. I get there a bit early, got a decent seat and a glass of Dutch courage to calm my nerves. I was halfway through my second bag of pork scratchings when the door opens... And there he is. All 5ft 2 of him. Bald as a coot. The photo he sent must have been taken when 'Culture Club' we're still in the charts. So I'm sat there panicking and thinking ' can I still fit through the toilet cubicle window?' So I go to stand up and just as I reach down to grab my bag he spots me and smiles, showing all four teeth he's got left in his head.

BEAUTY

Oh no... I'm starting to palpitate just thinking about it. What did you do??

SNOW

What could I do? I didn't have the guts to tell him to bugger off so I sat there counting the minutes till I could escape, nursing my warm rose and avoiding the clammy hand that kept gravitating towards my thigh! Never again. I'm staying away from online dating, no one is actually who they say they are on there!

LUM

I met someone out of the Friday add lonely hearts column once. Nice girl. We arranged to get together in a local bar and share a ploughman's. It was all going really well until I got a bit animated telling her one of my famous banquet stories and ended up setting her hair on fire. I had to throw a perfectly good pint of Guinness over her head to put it out. Strangely enough I never heard from her again ...

CRU

OH darling... Online dating is so passé. Just cut out the middle man and head to Maidstone. It's all happening there.

ROBIN

What's in Maidstone apart from a few bad shops?

CRU

A very long gravel drive leading to a fantastically discreet house dahh-ling. *(Silence)*

You can be anyone you want to be... For a fee.

ROBIN

What the hell is she talking about? Has she been sniffing the kitty litter again?

BEAUTY

I may me wrong, but I think she may be talking about swinging.

ROBIN

Ah... Been there done that.

LUM

Have you??

ROBIN

Yes... Kind of.

LUM

Well?

ROBIN

Well. I was sat in Weatherspoons one rainy evening last year and you know how they don't to play any music in there so you can hear every-one's conversations? *(LUM nods)*. So I was sat chewing the fat with a few of the merry men and there's three blokes sat behind us, all talking about going 'robbin' in Fairlight. So we bided our time & we waited until they left the pub and then followed them... From a distance... The idea was to let them do all the hard work then relieve them of their booty.

LUM

and did you?

ROBIN

Well there was certainly booty there but not the kind I was anticipating. They led us to a car park in the middle of bloody nowhere out in the country. At first I thought it was an ambush. But then one of the blokes drops his pants in front of a Ford Fiesta and some wench in the passenger seat winds her window down and starts to touch him up!! Turns out I'd misheard.., they weren't going robbin.., they were going doggin!!

(CHARMING starts to listen and look uncomfortable while doing the exercises)

LUM

Bloody hell. Where was this again? *(Gets a pad out of his bag)* Just So I know to avoid it....

ROBIN

I was just about to make a run for it when an engine roars into life behind me and suddenly I'm like a deer caught in the headlights! The merry men were nowhere to be seen. And then this car starts to creep up beside me... Black Beamer type thing. Tinted windows... And the window slowly winds down...

(CHARMING freezes! The class tries to stay in the pose)

LUM

And... And??

ROBIN

I couldn't really see her face... Big hat.... Blonde hair *(charming touches his own hair with a panic stricken face)* dark glasses. She reached through the window, unzips my pants and leans out and gives me the best blow job I've ever had in my life in the middle of a bloody car park!

LUM No!!

ROBIN
Yes!! No small talk. No 'so what would you like to drink... Or do you come here often' *(nudges LUM)*
It was great! *(pause)* She didn't half have had big hands mind you.

CHARMING *(looks at his hands... Gags and rushes to the toilet)* 'Excuse me!!

LUM
So... Have you been back since?

ROBIN
Yeah, the following night actually. I walked over there when it was dark and dropped my pants in front of a Mercedes sport... and... Unfortunately got arrested on the spot. Some old dear had parked up there for the county finals bridge meeting. She didn't half get a shock when my ace card appeared through her window in all its glory I can tell you.

(They all sit in various stages of disgust and awe)

CRU
Where's CHARMING buggered off too?

BEAUTY
He's nipped to the loo I think?

CRU
Well I hope he isn't long I've got a manicure at 12 and a lunch date with Pinocchio. He's turned into quite the ladies man. His nose isn't the only thing that grows when he lies. And he lies a lot to me...

BEAUTY
One of my online regulars wanted to meet me. You know... In the flesh.

SNOW
Really? Are you going too?

BEAUTY

I'm thinking about it... he seems really nice. Lovely face, tall, slim, likes the same flavoured yogurts as me. He's only got one hand though... I think he feels a bit self conscious about it to be honest

CRU

HOOK?? Your meeting hook? You can't meet hook? You're not his type!! He's an absolute cad! I cooked dinner for him a few months back...

ROBIN

I thought you never eat?

CRU

Just because I don't eat it doesn't mean I don't entertain sweetie, my Dalmatian stew is legendary! He seemed completely smitten, stroked my pussy throughout dessert and she hates being touched.
Polished off three bottles of my finest Beaujolais, & laughed at my jokes. Kissed me goodbye. & promised to take me for a day out on his galleon.
Never heard a word from him since

BEAUTY

I don't think that's the same chap. He told me his name was Duncan. He likes antiques and fly fishing and countdown.

CRU

Has he the hair the colour of a Raven? Eyes like coal? A dimple on his left cheek and a bloody great big silver hook on the end of his left wrist?

BEAUTY

Erm... Yes

CRU

Then wake up and smell the freshly baked cookies sweetie. Of course it's him! You can't meet him. I forbid it

BEAUTY

I beg your pardon?

CRU

I said. I forbid you to see him!

SNOW

I really don't think you can tell BEAUTY who she does and doesn't see...

CRU

I'm sorry... What has this got anything to do with you? Haven't you got some washing to do or some birds to sing too

LUM

Now, now ladies let's not make this personal...

CRU

Oh now the giant wick is getting involved. You can wax lyrical all you like but if you don't want me to snuff you out forthwith may I suggest you go and hide your light under somebody else's bushel and stay out of my business!

ROBIN

(To Lumiere) Oooh this is definitely more interesting than the Speed awareness course! My money is on the fruity one sporting the HRT patches. Those menopausal women have a worse temper than the wicked witch of the west does when she's sporting a house as a hat!

LUM

(Angry) May I suggest you take a long look in Snow's mirror Miss De-Vil before you continue with your venomous tongue. I'm afraid every dog has its day and if you were of the canine persuasion then the vet would have put you out of your misery a long time ago.

(ROBIN slaps LUM on the back. Keeps his arm there. LUM looks pleased with this new found camaraderie)

CRU

I have never been so insulted in my life!

BEAUTY

Then maybe you should get out more. I've spent my life cow towing to people like you and you know what? I'm fed up of it. If I want to fuck hook I jolly well will do so and you and your shrivelled up pussy can go choke on a hair ball.

SNOW (*laughs*)

CRU

(*To Snow*) I'm glad you find this amusing you dried up old prune. With a personality like yours no wonder old Princy walked out and left you to bring the sprogs up alone. No one over the age of 21 should be allowed out in puff sleeves. Even Gok Wan would have his work cut out with you. May I suggest you don't walk too close to LUMIERE when you leave or you'll all be going up in a puff of smoke? Now I'd love to stay & chat but I have an appointment with a nail technician.

(*CRU Goes to leave*)

SNOW

How dare you. How dare you come in here and tell us how we should live our lives.

So what if my dress sense isn't to your liking. At least I don't smell like wet dog. I may not have a man but I have four children who love me.

Who loves you CRU? Apart from your knocked up old pussy.

At least forehead still moves and I don't rattle when I walk. You have more poison running through your veins than any apple I've ever had the misfortune to bite into. May I suggest you go and get your talons sharpened without any more vitriol & I sincerely hope you and your scratching post will be very happy together. No wonder hook walked away from you. I've seen more warmth in a frozen Vienetta. Now fuck off and leave us all to our happy ever after!

End of Act 1. To be continued.

ABOUT THE AUTHOR

Paula Leskovitz

Having avoided a 'proper job' throughout her adult life, Paula has managed to travel the globe with only £4.67 in her bank account and humour as her trusted companion. From selling sandwiches to prostitutes in SOHO to waking up in a strangers bunk bed 6000 miles from home, encountering the rich and famous en route in the most unexpected of places, her life has been everything apart from ordinary.

There are many more tales to be told and certainly more tales to tell...

Printed in Great Britain
by Amazon

77844298R00108